A SPLINTER OF THE CROSS

by Vicki Flynn

Flynn & Flynn Enterprises, LLC

A Splinter of the Cross

©Vicki Flynn

ISBN 978-0-578-47932-3

First Edition

Cover Art by Lynn Smith

*I dedicate this book to my husband, Kevin.
Thank you for never letting go of my hand
in the darkness.*

Setting the Precedent

How do we spiritually digest the dysfunctional group that was Jonestown? We learn from the mistake. We see and heed the warning signs. We think for ourselves and take back our right to go to the Lord for any life direction. We take responsibility for our lives and their outcomes.

No, this is not a book about Jonestown or Jim Jones. But the roots of this church, the church I am about to introduce to you and the beginning of The People's Temple, the church that Jim Jones founded, are intertwined together. Jim Jones ministered with one of the founding fathers of the New Order of Latter Rain churches, William Branham. You will read more about him as you begin to unravel the sobering attributes...of a cult.[5]

You are about to embark on a journey of discovery. You will discover the significance of the beguiling thread that began with one leader - to the fabric that it creates by another leader in the following years of dysfunction and heresy.

Why is what one man considered as doctrine significant? Because he created an inertia that continues to this day. William Branham - an instrumental influence that began Latter Rain - was a "prophet." Because of the signs and wonders he produced through his "angel" he was taken seriously by Pentecostal circles.

The heresy he created still lives in what is left of the Latter Rain churches. His beliefs and doctrines are in the movements that were influenced by Latter Rain in the last part of the twentieth century until today. Remember, the characteristics of heretical, even evil influence is the

---

5 https://en.wikipedia.org/wiki/William_M._Branham

twisting of truth not the presentation of an outright lie.

If you have not experienced the deception of a cult, take heed. This is a warning. If you find yourself in the midst of loss...the loss of the ability to think for yourself, the loss of family and especially the loss of who you are, this book may help you regain your personal direction.

The process of a cult continues to where the individual is swept along in a current too strong for them to fight. They gradually defer all decisions to the leadership and in the end, it is ironic the following sentence is spoken to a man, instead of God. "It is not my will, but thine be done..."

Not all cults go to the *extreme* of physical death that Jonestown did. But, there are spiritual deaths. There is a commitment that you are required to make to God. This commitment is submission to the leadership. The "mind set" created by the leader of the cult takes over. You are bound by your commitment not to question. Then all your hopes, dreams and aspirations are destroyed. The leader has taken over your personal relationship with Jesus Christ. You will answer to him rather than the Lord. Your future will reflect the leader's desires, not your own.

When you find yourself trying to reason why you should leave, the "program" that has been created plays in your head, "The leadership knows best. We have committed our lives to them before God. If we disobey them, we disobey God. We'll dwell in outer darkness."

Hopefully, the following chapters will either prevent you from the path of allowing yourself to sacrifice what and Who you know or will provide a life map for you to come out of the darkness and deception of where you find yourself trapped.

What may be the alternative if you do not take back your life? Listen to the desperate cries of one who had finally come to the end of all his aspirations and contorted dreams.

[6] "Quickly! Quickly! Quickly! Quickly! Quickly! Where is the vat? The vat, the vat....Bring it here, so the adults can begin."

[6]https://www.scribd.com/document/135552376/**Jonestown-Transcript**

Chapter One

Our Present Torment

The sky was a deep azure blue, with huge white cumulus clouds floating in slow motion across the heavens, careful not to block the sun. A gentle, constant breeze gave assurance that the warmth of May was perfect. Moving to the touch of the wind, the meadow grass swayed with a rhythm all its own.

The mountains rose far into the blue back drop standing as disciplined sentries and we sat in the midst of them as the field gave itself as a berth, offering comfort and solitude.

The attempt of God's creation, to bring solace was a generous yet futile effort. The anguish and pain that riddled our souls overtook peace and we lay there, waiting for the very hand of God to reach down and stifle our cries.

Together, yet alone, we looked into each other's eyes, searching for some light of reason, anything to come forth from our severed, wounded thoughts. I looked down at the patterns in the quilt we were sitting on, then to the wild flowers growing in the meadow. Cognizance touched my confused, stunned mind. It was true. As much as we tried to deny and pretend, the inevitable was there. Reality was the victor and all hope was lost........They were gone.

Twenty-Three Years Earlier

"We are not necessarily doubting that God will do the best for us; we are wondering how painful the best will turn out to be."

C.S. Lewis[7]

[7]http://www.goodreads.com/quotes/615-we-are-not-necessarily-doubting-that-god-will-do-the

We were living in a small southern town, in an older but nice house, in a good neighborhood. We had only been married three years. We had our two beautiful girls and a garden. Life was good. Kevin was working for a fledgling company when another job opportunity came available. It was a promising position with a large, well - known northern corporation.

I was totally blindsided. Kevin had been looking for another job because the site where he worked was closing. He had not wanted to worry me, so this was a shock. Not only were we possibly moving, but we were moving to this particular city. I had sworn I would never move there, but God seemed to be opening doors. I've now learned not to say "never". The Lord just might want to confirm His Lordship in your life.

Kevin had been praying about what to do. That's how we prayed back then, "Lord if it be Your will, please either open or close the door, so we will know it is of You."

The interview process moved along quickly, and we were soon asked to fly up for a meeting with the proposed boss. Two nights before we were scheduled to leave, one of Kevin's front teeth broke off and he had to make an emergency visit to the dentist the next day. (Never go to an interview toothless.) The tooth was temporarily affixed until further work could be done. We were relieved and thought all was well.

Our girls were going to stay with my friends, the house was clean, and clothes were pressed into suitcases. Our agenda was moving along smoothly. We flew out early the next day.

The interview was scheduled for Sunday morning. On

Friday night, Kevin's face began to swell and became very painful. What we didn't know then, was that the dentist had sealed an abscessed tooth. Infection was spreading to his jaw and up near his eye.

He kept saying it was no big deal, but, after some excruciating hours on Saturday, he finally agreed to go to the hospital.

We were with a realtor at the time and she took us to the emergency room at one of the local hospitals. They gave him something for pain and sent him on his way.

By nightfall he was worse and that's when I knew that whatever this was would not be going away without major medical help.

There we were in a strange, dark city alone. I remember looking out at the lights from the ninth- floor window of our hotel as I was trying to decide what to do. At first, these sparkling lights seemed to be stalwart beacons of hope. They were so beautiful, shining through the darkness into our room, yet hope was only an illusion. There was no one out there behind those lights. There was no one whom I could call upon, no one to give me advice. I prayed, "Lord please help us. Please show us where to go, what to do and how to get there."

Finally, we knew we had to take action. Kevin was getting worse, so we made our way down to the lobby then out onto the street. I hailed a taxi for the first time in my life and the driver became a tangible link to finally receiving some help. We told him we needed to get to the ER. He asked which ER? We didn't have a clue, so we trusted him to pick one. I think he took the long way, his meter clicking away. It seemed like the ride took forever.

Being from out of town how would we have known? He wouldn't be the last to take advantage of our vulnerable and trusting nature.

At the hospital, Kevin was treated, temporarily. There were no oral surgeons in the ER, so they gave him some antibiotics and Demerol then we took another taxi back to the hotel.

Interestingly, the ride was much shorter. Kevin had been given the pain medication intravenously and by the time I got him to the hotel he could barely stand. Somehow, I got him back to our room and into the bed, praying the whole time. I think angels helped to carry him. I sat down by his side relieved that we had found help, took his hand and thanked the Lord. Mercifully, he slept through the night.

The next morning, despite of the way he looked, with the right side of his face swollen to triple its normal size, he made it downstairs for the interview and got the job. I think his new boss took pity on him. It all happened so fast. It was a go!

I was having a tug of war with my emotions. Moving North had not been an aspiration of mine. I was afraid of the winters. I was afraid of the culture. I was afraid of the unknown. I wasn't just from the South, I was from the Heart of Dixie, as southern as they come. Growing up, the word "Yankee" had been spoken in my presence more than once in a derogatory way. My daddy even had a poster of a cartoon Confederate soldier with the words, "Forget Hell!" in his office.

As Kevin and I planned what to do next, we tried to take comfort in telling each other, that what the enemy had meant for harm, God meant for good. After all, Kevin had gotten the job, hadn't he? Wasn't that an open door?

We flew home that afternoon. We were running late and hadn't timed the drive to the airport correctly. Kevin drove like a maniac. We had to run to the gate. Of course, it was at the very end of the terminal. I ran ahead of Kevin to hold the door. I don't know how he could run at all. We barely made the flight.

When we landed I drove home as fast as I could with Kevin "holding on" beside me. I picked up a few things and we went straight to the hospital. The emergency room doctor admitted him right away. The infection was heading toward his brain for goodness sake! We never saw "that" dentist again.

With oral surgery, IV antibiotics and some rest in the hospital for a few days, he began his recovery. We started packing for our move as soon as he got home.

The company paid for Kevin and me to fly up for a weekend to find a place to live. I was actually excited and looked forward to finding our new home. We didn't know anything about the area, but we knew what part of the city we wanted to live in. It was a suburb south of Kevin's work and we only had two days to sign a lease.

Nothing was working out until we looked at the very last place. It was a quaint house in a quaint neighborhood and we scrambled to get the paper work done before we had to fly out. The owner seemed to be very nice, we loved the area, the public school was right up the street and we would be close to Kevin's work. It was a done deal. Another door had been opened just in the nick of time.

Sometimes the door is shut for a reason and "we" tend to offer more than a little nudge to open it.

Chapter Two

It Begins

Cast the burden of the present, along with the sin of the past and the fear of the future, upon the Lord, who forsaketh not his saints.

— *Charles Spurgeon* [8]

It was a gorgeous, crisp, clear fall morning. I have to admit the colors of the seasons were always beautiful in the north. We were finally on our way to church. We had been looking for a church for a couple of months after our move. Due to our Southern roots, the churches we had visited in the area, seemed stiff and liturgical. We were looking for something new and exciting like the first church in the book of Acts.

We were looking for signs and wonders, spiritual manifestations and fireworks. The Lord is very specific about those who seek after the excitement of signs and supernatural experiences versus having enough faith to believe in Him without them.

Jesus Appears to Thomas — John 20: 24 - 29

[24]Now Thomas (also known as Didymus[a]), one of the Twelve, was not with the disciples when Jesus came. [25]So the other disciples told him, "We have seen the Lord!" But he said to them, "Unless I see the nail marks in his hands and put my finger where the nails were, and put my hand into his side,I will not believe." [26]A week later his disciples were in the house again, and Thomas was with

[8]http://www.reclaimingthemind.org/blog/2014/04/quotes-from-the-valley-of-the-shadow-of-death-charles-spurgeon-1834-1892/

them. Though the doors were locked, Jesus came and stood among them and said,"Peace be with you!"²⁷ Then he said to Thomas,"Put your finger here; see my hands. Reach out your hand and put it into my side. Stop doubting and believe." ²⁸Thomas said to him, "My Lord and my God!"

²⁹ *Then Jesus told him,"Because you have seen me, you have believed; blessed are those who have not seen and yet have believed."*

Do I believe in signs and wonders? Absolutely. Are they necessary to have a vital relationship with the Lord? Absolutely not. I have learned this lesson the hard way.

We stayed home from going to church one Sunday, a little discouraged, and watched church on television at home. The pastor said, "Even if you have to look in the phonebook to find a church, that's what you need to do."

I went straight to the kitchen and pulled out the Yellow Pages. I looked for any name that sounded familiar to the section of the township we lived in. I finally found a church that was in our area.

I picked up the phone and dialed the number. I called during the time of the church service and I really didn't expect anyone to answer. However, a very pleasant-sounding woman answered on the other end. She fielded all our basic questions regarding their doctrine. She was positive and sincere.

Did they believe Jesus was the Son of God? Did He die on the cross to forgive us of our sin and make a way for eternal life? Did they believe in the Trinity? Did Mary have a virgin birth? Did they believe the Bible was the unadulterated Word of God? All her answers were, "Yes." We were excited about visiting somewhere that seemed to be like minded with our beliefs.

The following Sunday when we met her, she and her husband welcomed us with open arms and seemed truly thrilled that we were there. This kind of welcome was foreign to us, even in the South.

She soon became one of my closest friends and was literally like a sister to me. She once vowed that she *would* be my sister and would always be there if I needed anything. We had many "all-night" conversations when we got together for a visit and over the years found that we had become more than just sisters. We were kindred spirits.

Being our first visit to the church, we were ushered into the sanctuary, which was a gym with a platform added in the front and chairs set up for the congregants. We asked to be seated in the back. Since it was our first visit, we wanted to be inconspicuous in case we didn't want to visit again.

After a phenomenal praise and worship experience, where you literally felt you were caught up into the heavenlies, everyone sat back down in their chair. The pastor began to read the announcements. At that point of the service, our feet planted back firmly on solid ground, the atmosphere changed. It was more casual, more personable. We had been spotted and were purposely made to feel welcomed.

"We have some visitors with us today!" Our names were called out. Then the pastor asked smiling," What brings you here this morning?"

"A job," my husband responded. To our chagrin, the pastor and the whole congregation laughed.

"A job - huh?" the pastor said. We were taken aback. Why was everyone laughing?

"Welcome. It is good to have you here," the pastor offered.

After the service, the pastor and a lot of the members came up to shake our hands and introduce themselves. We were even invited to someone's home for lunch for the following Sunday. On the way home we realized why everyone laughed. They laughed because they believed the divine hand of the Lord had brought us there, not a job.

Kevin and I could believe that. We *wanted* to believe that. We swallowed the spiritual flattery hook, line and sinker. It made sense to us because it appealed to our hunger for spiritual manifestations of God's will, at the time. We had already made a long-range goal to stay with Kevin's new job for five years then move on up the career ladder. So, it was settled. For as long as we would be living in that city, we had found a church.

Chapter Three

Handled with Kid Gloves

The "honeymoon" phase lasted for a while. Everyone went above and beyond being friendly. Within the first couple of weeks, we found out the pastor was actually called the "apostle". We were startled and concerned about someone receiving this title in the day and time we lived in.

I called one of the ladies who had been kind enough to give me her number. I didn't wait for niceties to be exchanged. I asked her point blank how this could be possible. After several minutes of laying out a doctrine that was supported by scripture, she concluded that there were authentic, modern day apostles.

When I hung up the phone, I reasoned that maybe I didn't fully understand the Bible to the level of spirituality that she had attained. I really hadn't studied scripture specifically concerning apostles. Basically, what she said calmed my apprehension When I shared her explanation with Kevin, he was relieved too.

The second Sunday we were there, the "apostle" made statements from the pulpit, challenging our born again experience. He basically said that just because you had repented didn't mean you were "born again' or that "salvation" had taken place. You were only justified – another startling moment.

I later realized that what he preached the first two to three months we were there didn't just happen to be a sermon he would preach on any Sunday morning. It was always tailor made for us. We were new and had to "learn the ropes." His self-assured, charismatic nature had already caught our attention. We learned later that everything he said was for a purpose. Nothing random ever came out of his mouth.

Well, being the strong willed, assertive southern lady, I was, I believed this apostle was casting a sooty shadow on the unadulterated light of the Gospel. That following Monday morning I was on the phone as fast as a duck on a June bug. I wanted to know exactly what he meant by "insinuating" we weren't born again!

I was used to pastors being hired by the church and therefore subject to the congregation's needs. My experience with denominational churches was they were run by their organizations, with the members being represented by deacons. I was used to being heard when I made a phone call to the pastor.

He took my call right away and was very cordial and even gracious with me, answering all my questions. I later learned that Monday was his day off and members were not allowed to call or bother him on his day of rest. I also soon found out that in no way was this man a hireling, far from it.

He recommended that my husband and I start attending his Christian education class, for new people, where all my questions would be answered. He said, "That will give you the opportunity to get to know us, and we will be able to get to know you. It works both ways, you see." That seemed a little different, but I didn't dwell on it.

By the time I got off the phone, I was no longer upset. What he had told me seemed to make perfect sense. I was in a trance following every idea of doctrine that he laid out. I ignored the alarm that had been sounding inside my head. After all, he was an apostle for heaven's sake, someone that must really know a lot about the Bible!

I told Kevin that the apostle had said being born again happens in three stages – justification, water baptism and baptism of the Holy Spirit. He had scripture to back up everything he said, I explained.

So, Kevin and I talked about the idea of attending the class and believed that maybe we had found something, something different". We started attending the Christian education class and began to relearn a lot of the doctrine we believed. We had been wrong, you see. According to the apostle and his revelation, we only knew part of the plan of salvation. We were told we would never see the "Kingdom of God" until we were truly born again. The class and the material used, would teach us just how to go about doing that.

Sure, I had heard the phrase "Kingdom of God" before. But this was different. What did everybody mean? It was mysterious, something that was unattainable unless you followed the "pattern". That's why we were taking the class. We couldn't see the full picture, yet we pressed on. The pattern, we wanted to know what that meant.

We were like mice in a maze. We were running blindly, searching for the next reward or manifestation of something new, something exciting. Now, we had been given something to attain.

The man who taught the Christian education class, when the apostle was absent, (which was often) was an elder in the church, a very gracious and loving man. Our girls would go to church with us. The eldest would sit in the congregational meeting, that was going on simultaneously, with friends and our youngest would go to the nursery.

The teacher and his wife would often have us over after class to answer any questions we had about the teaching. She would serve pie and coffee and our children would play with theirs. He would answer all our questions favorably and we would go home satisfied. We were settling in and were ready to extend some hospitality.

He came to visit us one night at our home while we were taking the class, the apostle. I offered coffee, the house was spotless, and conversation was going well. I decided to take a moment to tell him what my spiritual gift was. I guess I was trying to impress him.

I told him I had the gift of mercy. (Romans: 12:6-8) I was thankful and felt blessed for that gift. The Lord had allowed me to use it numerous times.

But go and learn what this means: 'I desire mercy, not sacrifice.' For I have not come to call the righteous, but sinners. Matthew 9:13

When I told him about my gift, I got a response that totally took me aback. He said, "Ohhhh, be careful! People can take advantage of you with that gift – if you give them an excuse, they won't change." I was speechless. Won't change? Change into what? What did that mean?

I felt like I had been punched in the stomach, as though I had done something wrong. How could following scripture be wrong? I was embarrassed, even ashamed. I wanted to take those words, put them right back in my mouth and swallow them.

"There are people who go after your humanity. Who tell you the light in your heart is a weakness. Don't believe it. It is an old tactic of cruel people to kill kindness in the name of virtue. There is nothing wrong with love. Have you forgotten the message of our Savior – Love for the people."

Father Kevin Flynn – from the movie <u>Doubt</u> [5]

I never spoke about my gift again. That moment cut deep into my spirit suppressing any mercy that was left inside of me. Not until I heard the above quote years later, did I realize what I had lost. Sobbing, I realized I had been on the right path. That path was blocked by the apostle's words and I was forced to take a detour – a detour into apathy.

We faithfully attended the classes every Sunday night for nine months. During this period of time, when everything was new and interesting, I was invited over to a lady's home for tea. She had other ladies there, as well, so I could get to know them better. It wasn't long before the subject of the "Kingdom of God" came up in the conversation. I had questions and was asking what makes this phrase so important?

No one was really answering my questions. The conversation seemed to be going around in circles. I was getting a little frustrated.

The apostle's daughter-in-law took me aside and told me that once I was baptized, my eyes would be opened, and I would truly see what the Kingdom of God was all about.

There had been sermons lately about the parable of

"the pearl of great price" (Matthew 13:46). With all this intrigue, I felt like I was going on a treasure hunt.

Another word was being spoken quite often that intrigued Kevin and me. This word was "remnant" and we heard it from the pulpit and from the people that we were meeting and getting to know. Remnant didn't need an explanation. It was very evident what it meant.

The apostle taught that the members of this church were a part of the remnant, the chosen ones. Those who belonged were part of an elitist crowd. Being a part of the remnant was more than what the nominal Christian believed.

We wanted to be part of the remnant. We wanted to be in the company of those who were going to "make it".

But just like the "Kingdom of God," being a part of the remnant had to be obtained. We had to follow the *pattern*. The nine-month class was genius. We went through each topic slowly, methodically. The one on one sessions with our teacher were putting all our doubts and questions to rest. We were gradually being indoctrinated into becoming a part of the *remnant*.

You couldn't become a member of the church until you graduated from the class. And you couldn't graduate from the class until you were baptized/re-baptized in Jesus' name for "the remission of your sins and the circumcision of your heart". The baptism had to be performed by someone who was in leadership and had been baptized the same way. That person had to impart to you the correct pattern.

(This Oneness doctrine of being baptized in Jesus' name is a carryover from one of the founders of Latter Rain – who proclaimed that the Trinitarian doctrine [Father, Son and Holy Spirit] "was of the devil")

Also, you needed to have received the baptism of the Holy Spirit with evidence of speaking in tongues. Otherwise, you were not truly born again in their minds and you could not enter the "Kingdom of God."

I had already been baptized at least three times through all the different denominations I experienced, and I had received what they called the baptism of the Holy Spirit. So, had Kevin. But according to this church, baptism was not just another way of being obedient to the Lord's commandment, part of joining the church or a way of demonstrating your faith. It was the key to your salvation, not just the declaration of it. It was your entry into the New Covenant.

According to the apostle, we came out of the water, having entered the "Kingdom of God" and found out in the coming months that we were on our way to "ruling and reigning" with Christ in the New Jerusalem.

Not many Christians understood the"truth" the way we understand it, he would say to his congregation . Those people were "nominal" Christians. We were becoming "sons".

The pattern had now been set before us and we ended up following not a method...but a man.

Chapter Four

Caught in the Rain
(A Glimpse Behind the Curtain)

... there are some who are disturbing you and want to distort the gospel of Christ.

Galatians 1:7

The nine months of taking the class were finally over. We had taken and passed all the tests, written and otherwise. We had covered all the doctrine and most of it was directly tied to the Latter Rain Movement of the 1940's.

Latter Rain affected our church services, our doctrine, our method of raising our children and our very lives.

The Latter Rain movement began in 1948 at Sharon Orphanage in Saskatchewan, Canada. The initial phenomenon of praise, worship and prophesy was founded there.

George Hawtin (1909-1994) - was a key leader of the "New Order of Latter Rain."He was excommunicated in 1960 because he saw the fruit of the movement and wasn't afraid to tell what he saw. His words sum up what happened during the early years and how "man" took over:

"...as I look sadly in retrospect now, I can see with clearness that the great and blessed move of God was not two years old before the sectarian (fanatical, schismatic) spirit began to show its ugly head...it is true that we vociferously (shouted, loudly) denied that we had become a sect... [6]

---

[6] kingdom-resources.com/category/george-r-hawtin/

The very fact that we were convinced to be baptized again took away our personal stance of believing that God had already done a work in us, through justification alone: forgiveness by the accepted sacrifice of Jesus so that we may inherit eternal life and a right relationship with God the Father.

We gave in to a distorted doctrine, that has been "flatly" interpreted by men who take the cross for granted and in turn hold water baptism the necessary tenet to enter the New Covenant.

We were changing, and we didn't even realize it. Our whole life was being inundated not only with how they interpreted the scripture but how they interacted with people. There was an air of superiority about them and if we wanted to *advance* in the "Kingdom of God," we were told to emulate everything they did. We were turning into who they expected us to be. The Lord was disappearing into the distance.

The magnificent salvation that we once received, of being sought after and found by our Lord Jesus Christ, that we had been cleansed of all our sin through His blood He shed on the cross, experiencing His love and sacrifice for **us**, so that we could fellowship with God the Father, His Father, throughout eternity, had been reduced to one word...justification.

Their interpretation was just that we could now stand before God and not be guilty of our sin. There was no relationship involved. It was an extraneous word compared to the "rest of their Gospel." It was a stepping stone of the mundane to get to the "supernatural."

Graduation from the class was all pomp and

circumstance. Part of the ceremony involved the graduates committing themselves to the apostle and elders, their leadership and to the church body.

In return, the apostle spoke for the church and committed themselves to the graduate. There was a word that was spoken in our commitment that was not reciprocated.

That word was *obey*.

The church also had a school for the children, open to members only. We didn't think much about that at the time. There were plenty of children to fill the classrooms, so we viewed the school as a service to the members.

We were excited about enrolling our oldest daughter in the school. She had been going to a public school the previous year and was bullied mercilessly. The bullies capitalized on the fact that she was from the south and teased her about her clothes, her long blonde hair, and her accent. I had met with her teacher trying to make the bullying go away. But it was to no avail.

We started her in the church school the next fall. I volunteered in the class rooms a few days a week. It was mandatory if you had a child enrolled in the school. Some of the teachers were paid a modest salary. Everyone else was considered a volunteer.

(Latter Rain doctrine was well established as a part of the school, as well as the church and was repeatedly woven into all the member's spiritual psyches, including the children.

Obedience was tantamount. If we wanted to obey the Lord, we had to obey the "apostle's" teachings. This doctrine was integrated into us quickly. Members of the church would subtly ingrain words and phrases in our conversations, letting us know that the apostle was the ultimate authority.

The apostle's wife was the school principal and was the ultimate authority there. Corporal punishment was used when the children didn't obey. Orange slips were given out frequently for any omission regarding homework. Yellow slips were sent out to comment on behavior. Many students were labeled, put in a box and were never given the benefit of the doubt. Partiality was evident, depending where you stood on the ladder of leadership.

I experienced some of this intimidation first hand. But I heard stories from other parents who suffered so much more with this type of "bullying" than I did. The only difference between this school and the public school was the age of the bullies.

To the child's detriment the bullies were the adults: teachers, classroom aides and most importantly the principal. To be sure, there were bullies among the students, and we were told to teach our children to let their words roll off, like water off a duck's back. A class distinction began to be apparent at this point. If the child of an elder was picked on, the offending student was punished severely.

There was also a nursery for moms who had little ones, pre- kindergarten. There were times that children with bad colds were allowed in the nursery so that enough volunteers were present to keep the school running. Flu (stomach and respiratory), strep throat, or chicken pox epidemics would break out regularly. The apostle's wife was a nurse and should have known better. I believe she did know better.

I remember making an appointment with the principal (apostle's wife) during the first year we attended the church.

Before marrying Kevin, I had been married to an abusive husband and still had some baggage from that relationship. I was even having bad dreams. After I told her why I was having nightmares, I couldn't say another word. She talked the entire time. I really didn't have much of a problem, I found out. She spoke about herself, her own problems and accomplishments.

I discovered quickly that feelings, emotions and sentiments were taboo. My feelings about this past relationship weren't important. The mantra that I learned that day was, "What is the truth?"

I used that twisted phrase of spiritual warfare for the rest of the time I was involved with this church.

Whenever anyone in the congregation felt tangible, valid emotions that alluded to being "dismissed" as a person by the apostle and his wife, they were told to ask themselves, "What is the truth?" If we began to have doubts about doctrine or the school, the apostle and leadership would say, "What is the truth?" The "truth" was always what the apostle said it was.

In spite of misgivings of the apostle's definition of the truth and our experiences with the school, it wasn't long before we found ourselves wanting to please him and his wife. We wanted them to be proud of us.

They had the members call them "Mom" and "Dad". They wanted to take that place of authority and control in our lives. This dysfunctional give and take seemed normal. It was a dance of co-dependency.

Ministry was the destination many were aiming for, the Shangri - la where we could become an integral part of the church. *We* wanted to attain to some sort of ministry. Then, in our minds, we would be considered worthy.

Kevin and I had both come from dysfunctional backgrounds. We had started attending here on a quest for something to make us feel complete, something different. Now, not only did we want something *new*, we wanted to be praised for finding *it*.

The teachings of Latter Rain involved the "apostle" having a direct line to God and he was not to be questioned. Hebrews 13:17 – was used to help facilitate this directive along with other writings.

"Obey them that have the rule over you and submit yourselves: for they watch for your souls, as they that must give account, that they may do it with joy, and not with grief: for that *is* unprofitable for you." NKJV

Paul was an apostle. This pastor was an "apostle." Paul was planting churches. Respect and obedience were expected in regard to his teachings. This "apostle" was planting churches and teaching his doctrine. Get the picture? Yes, this man likened himself to Paul. He isn't and never was like Paul in any since of the word. Yet he was able to pull it off. He convinced everyone that he was.

He had an *air* about him of confidence and authority. We definitely saw through a glass darkly.

Our love and service for the Lord was being used against us. How? – Because, ultimately, we wanted to serve our Lord Jesus, to please *Him*. We never *wanted* to please a man. The apostle knew this. We were not being taught - but brain washed to believe that to be part of the remnant we had to follow the "pattern". To serve Jesus, we had to go through the "apostle." We truly believed that by doing this we were, in turn, pleasing the Lord – tragic

My extraordinary and life changing relationship with the Lord was on the line again. I had accepted the Lord Jesus as my Lord and Savior because I was utterly heartbroken, and realized, with the help of the Holy Spirit, what He had sacrificed for me, not because I was afraid of Hell.

The Passion of Christ, the beatings, the crown of thorns, the scourging with a whip that had straps six feet long, with pieces of metal or bone that would literally tear the flesh into strips, describes how He suffered *before* He ever went to the cross. I wanted to repay Him with my life for what He had done. And you know what? That was stolen from me.

We were vehemently discouraged from seeing the movie *The Passion of Christ*. But that wasn't all. Neither we nor our children were allowed to watch any movies with a rating above G. Nor were we to watch Disney movies. This was considered to be unfit for our standards of venerating those in authority. Books were banned as well. Relationships outside of members of the church were discouraged. Acquaintances from the workplace were only allowed if you brought them to church. Clubs outside of the confines of the church were suspect. Sports were deemed divisive because competition would foster wrong attitudes. Our lives and those of our children were to revolve solely around the church and its members.

Being sequestered behind four walls, forbidden to reach out to tell others what Jesus had done for me by dying on the cross, quenched my joy until I became a dogmatic, legalistic, judgmental pseudo-Christian, just like the leaders.

√ In this church, the fruit of the spirit; love, joy, peace, forbearance, kindness, goodness, faithfulness, gentleness and self-control were replaced by idolatry, superiority, discord, jealousy, fits of rage, selfish ambition, dissentions, factions, and envy. (from Galatians 5: 19 -23) NKJV

In addition to isolating us from outside information and relationships, other forms of manipulation were used as well. Directive prophetic meetings (the presbytery – from Latter Rain) were held once a year. The apostle, and whomever he invited to prophesy with him, would stand on the platform and deliver personal, predictive prophecies over a certain number of choice congregants. A list of chosen members was drawn up by the apostle to determine who would be participating. These members would have to be deemed worthy to receive prophetic direction. Couples were most often called up and proceeded onto the platform together. Occasionally singles were called.

The "five-fold ministries" mentioned in Ephesians 4: 11,12 – NKJV...

[11]And He Himself gave some *to be* apostles, some prophets, some evangelists, and some pastors and teachers, [12]for the equipping of the saints for the work of ministry, for the edifying of the body of Christ...

were what the congregants aspired to.

The fact that "gave" in this scripture is written in past tense was ignored and still is by many Charismatic and Pentecostal churches today.

Ministries were assigned to those on the list and futures were determined by these prophecies. The most desired ministry to be given and the one that was held in highest regard was "pastor". (Apostle was off the table. There already was one in our midst.)

The office of pastor was often held out in front of men like a carrot. If you were "called" to be a pastor that meant that your life path would be closer to the apostle's and his inner circle of other pastors and elders that were a part of the church. You would receive the benefit of being a disciple of the apostle himself. Grievously, this was not always the case.

The travesty of this ambition was that the men would do everything they could to please the apostle and seek his approval. Transference of allegiance from God to the apostle was prevalent throughout the whole church. If we could receive a nod, a hand shake, a smile from the apostle, we were then furthering ourselves into the church's interpretation of the "Kingdom of God." The Lordship of Jesus Christ continued to slowly disappear into a fog of deception as the focus on the authority and veneration of the apostle emerged.

We didn't know that behind the scenes of what seemed to be a very welcoming, Bible teaching church, was tainted by the Latter Rain Movement's ambition to edify man instead of God. We were about to witness what George Hawtin had witnessed but in a more contorted way. Latter Rain had birthed a full -fledged cult.

Kevin and I had been there maybe two and a half years when our names were written on the list for "Presbytery." We were in line to receive directive prophesy.

Testimonial from an Ex - Member -# 1

I was introduced to this church at the age of 10 when my parents moved our family over to the United States from England for about 18 months. My first impression was that everyone was very welcoming, and very giving. However, I also noticed that everyone seemed "poised" in every respect of the word, almost to a point of abnormal human behavior. I thought, "How could people be so perfect all the time?" My siblings and I attended the school that was under church oversight, and as time went on, I began to notice that this group of people only gathered together with their own church members. Children were discouraged from playing with "children on the outside". Having come in from "the outside" this was in stark contrast to what I grew up with. I had previously spent a significant amount of time with people who were missionaries, which I thought was appropriate for someone who was a believer in Christ. "How were we supposed to bring others to Christ?" Was the question that lingered in my mind.

I recall that any children that were new to the school were all placed one grade behind the grade that they were supposed to be in for their age. It seemed to me that it was assumed that they were "behind in their academics" because they did not start their education from that school. My siblings and I were all placed as such, regardless of the fact that my brother was always the top of his class in England... I don't recall any prior academic testing being done to determine the placement of a child into their education program either.

My family was always a very sociable family who had friends from all walks of life and from various places around the world. However, this experience with the church changed our thinking because not only could we "no longer fellowship with these people", my dad was even forbidden to continue to be friends with another pastor from a neighboring church of the same or similar belief system!! I remember my dad questioning this and his questioning was not only frowned upon but clearly, he felt forced into the "decision" to sever this friendship.

Upon moving back to England our connection with the church remained. During the next 10 years I flew over and visited about 3 or 4 different times staying with a good friend, who was of course a member of the church. At the age of 18, I had also started to correspond with the man who would become my husband, who again of course was from the church. I recall that during the time of our correspondence and after we had become engaged, the pastor/apostle was visiting our church in England. We were considered to be one of the "satellite churches" of the main church. I don't recall his exact reason for this visit, but I do recall him talking to me about what seemed to be the intention of discouraging me from marrying my now husband (of 22 years might I add). He "paid me a compliment" and told me that he would even be pleased to see me married to one of his own sons!!! (Oh **** NO!!) My then fiancé moved over to England in 1994 a month prior to our marriage. We were married and received many beautiful gifts from many members of *****. Sometime after we received these gifts and cards we began to receive MUCH criticism over the fact that we did not send thank you cards. The fact remains that sometime during the process of these items being brought over, the cards and gifts had become separated from one another and as we had more cards than gifts we were unsure as to who had sent what. Criticism was a common practice amongst any of the churches. It seemed that it was for the purpose of gaining some sort of emotional control over the individual. Many of the things that we observed were a sense of powerlessness from the member. If anyone so much as questioned the "church leadership" regarding pretty much anything, they were cast out and cut off from remaining church family members. The remaining family members were now not only forbidden to fellowship with their "outside family" but fear was used to make them remain in the church. They were brainwashed into believing that somehow their salvation was extremely conditional upon their remaining there. So many people are still hurting from this simply because they cannot see their family. It's as if their family has long since been deceased without the opportunity to say goodbye. Very painful.

One of the many things that I recall being indoctrinated into the young minds of the children that attended the school was, "they would never amount to anything. The "need" to always impress was great. "Your appearance was one that must always be of excellence". This was also an indoctrination regarding a lady's overall appearance. She was often told, "If the barn looks better painted, then paint it!!".

I recall sickness being regarded as "the result of a having a sinful nature". One of the members of ***** had moved over to England to marry within the "satellite church", some years later she was suffering with cancer and was dying, she and her husband flew over to Pittsburgh so that this lady might see her friends just one last time, she was not even permitted into the building. This was early 2005! My own father -in - law never attended the church as he immediately saw it for what it was. However, my mother – in - law attended, became a member and of course so did her children. The leadership at the church tried countless times to get my mother – in –law to divorce my father – in – law! Simply because he wasn't a member or as they would put it, she was "unequally yoked".

This is most of what I can recall about this place. Nothing of what happened here caused [7]anyone's life to improve, rather it caused the reverse of that, because too many people are hurting as a result of the damage done.

Thank you so much for allowing me to express my own recollections, I hope that families can be reunited as they should be and that those responsible be brought to some sort of justice. No one has the right to control the life of another for any reason!

Blessings

Chapter Five

Washing of the Brain

"Nothing teaches us about the preciousness of the Creator as much as when we learn the emptiness of everything else."

Charles Haddon Spurgeon [6]

We spent weeks praying about the directive prophesy meeting. We had witnessed one when it was held the year before. Two prophets from out of town came to prophesy with the apostle. He thought it would be more effective if the men didn't know the people personally who they were prophesying over.

There was no nursery held for presbyteries. Families would come with their little ones, blankets in tow to make a pallet on the floor for them to sleep on. Tupperware bowls full of Cheerios, bottles, sippy cups and quiet toys were brought with hopes that the children would remain distracted.

The year we received prophesy, there were pastors from the church and most of the other churches we were in fellowship with that attended. There were about eight pastors in all.

There was one pastor, in particular, from another country who Kevin and I had great respect for. When our names were called, and we were sitting on the platform, facing the congregation, he came up to me and said, "Ah, there you are. I saw a woman with a white blouse in my

[6]http://www.goodreads.com/quotes/615-we-are-not-necessarily-doubting-that-god-will-do-the

mind today when I was praying". I was wearing a white blouse.

The meeting began. The congregation was led into praise by the apostle. Some were praying in tongues, some in English, some both. This type of praise and worship was the prelude to any kind of ministry in the church.

When the voices died down the sanctuary was quiet for a few minutes. Then someone came forward and prophesied over Kevin. Each pastor took turns prophesying "words" over us. Some were directive, and some were encouraging. The session that involved the ultimate plan for our future went on for quite some time.

When everything was said and done, the office of pastor was the ministry that emerged from the "voice of the prophets." The implications of being a pastor were overwhelming. Yet, the calling that so many wished for was now ours. We walked around a little bewildered for a couple of weeks. We were "humbled". We had high expectations. We didn't have a clue. Our lives had changed so radically in just a few years. Our goals were different, our dreams were now submitted to the apostle. Our future was no longer ours.

Around this time, we were invited by the apostle to visit a church we were in fellowship with in another state. They were hosting a pastor's conference. One evening, everyone was sitting around the table eating and talking. We were meeting new people and I was talking with someone, telling them about myself. During the conversation, I said that I had changed. Immediately, I heard this voice from the other side of the table say, "Yes, you have." I turned toward the voice, a little startled. It was the apostle. He had an expression of pride on his face and I determined a sense of accomplishment. I blushed and went back to staring at my plate, speechless.

We were right on schedule as far as the apostle was concerned. The obstinate, forward, strong personality of a southern woman had been tamed. The woman who had called him on that Monday morning, questioning his preaching was gone.

Kevin was relying less and less on his career. His aspirations were disappearing into the fog of unyielding obedience. The "Kingdom of God" is where we put our hopes and strengths. It was the only place that was worthy – the apostle's paradigm of godliness.

One of the practices of the church was to cut off any friends or family who were not associated with any of the churches. This was to ensure that we wouldn't be lured away from the church through "normality." We were "told" it was because we were unequally yoked.

Over time, Kevin and I distanced ourselves from our families. We discontinued relationships with our friends. We took less trips down south and we focused on cultivating friends and family in the churches we were in fellowship with. He had been called to pastor. Ministry was on the line.

Whenever I would have lunch, or we would go out to dinner with the apostle and his wife she would always talk about how she cut her mother off and it was the best thing she could have ever done. Ironically, the apostle's mother attended the church and he and his sons took care of her needs until she passed. Later he talked about what a burden she had been.

The fact that our future vision changed so radically within such a short period of time definitely suggests the insidiousness of brainwashing. People ask, "How in the world did you get caught up in something like that?" By the time the cultish behavior was being revealed to us we were already brainwashed. We had learned the "pattern" and it continuously reverberated in our heads.

People will talk about the fact that they or someone they know has been brainwashed but they never tell you how. I believe this is a good time to take a break from the storyline to mention certain signs to look for.

I've done some research on the subject and I think you will find the points illuminating. I hope they will make you vigilant.

1. The mind is wiped clean -
   How does this happen? With us, it was the nine months of the Christian education class that wiped away all of our preconceived ideas about doctrine and interpretation of scripture. Then the apostle and his leadership replaced all of what was "washed" away with their dogma.

2. Lack of autonomy –
   You are coerced and encouraged to put your plans, career and dreams on hold for the "Kingdom of God". You must find out how you can be of service there, directly or indirectly.

3. Fear of missing the "Kingdom of God" –
   You are told that you will miss God's best for you and will not inherit your reward. Missing heaven altogether is inferred if you don't submit and follow the "pattern".

4. The apostle and his wife act as a parental role – You are told to call them Mom and Dad. There are emotional ties to these roles and they are used to gain allegiance.

5. You are told to cut off your friends and family – This is the most telling of all the indications of a cult. They want to isolate you, so you are influenced by them only. [8]

These are most of the ways you can be brainwashed but not all. They are the most obvious and therefore may be used as a guideline to keep tucked away in case there ever is a need.

Most importantly, if any of the preceding chapters are the least bit familiar, run away from where you are as fast as you can and never look back.

During this period of time in the church, the apostle wanted to create other avenues for stewards of whom he would have power over. It really wasn't about spreading the "good news" of the Kingdom. It was more for the purpose of adding notches to his spiritual measuring stick.

In addition to the above list, there is another insidious strategy that cult leaders use with their members. It's called "grooming". It is a gradual process. You have probably heard the allegory of the frog in a pot of water on the stove. The temperature is slowly turned up. The frog adjusts to this change until to his consternation, the water starts to boil.

In our case, we started to feel a part of that church from the very first Sunday we attended. Then, I was asked to

[8] http://www.wikihow.com/Recognize-and-Avoid-Brainwashing

attend a few ladies get togethers. We were asked to join the class that everyone had to take. The apostle sought us out after church to shake our hands.

I know this all sounds normal. Mostly, it is normal in a church where the Word of God isn't skewed. But the conversations that took place with the ladies were like those of college girls trying to make me pledge their sorority. They spoke about the Kingdom of God as if it was a mystical concept and there was only one way to enter.

The apostle started inviting us out to lunch after church. He and his wife would talk about situations of disobedience with a member and how they felt about it. He would tell us stories of how he had been hurt, emotionally, by different people. Compliments toward Kevin and me began.

They wanted us to call them Mom and Dad. He invited us to visit one of the churches that was out of the country with his wife and him. We paid our own way, but we still felt honored.

Within less than a year, Kevin and I wanted to be their champions. We especially wanted to protect *him*. We wanted to impress him... We wanted to *serve* him.

Really, it didn't take a whole lot to bring Kevin and me on board. We had been looking for something more, spiritual fireworks. Well, it had happened. We were now part of an exclusive, private club. Especially, we were the only ones who knew how to enter the Kingdom of God, be *truly* born again, and interpret the Bible correctly.

We were there five years before we were sent out to start our own church, under the apostle of course.

The apostle made an effort to teach a class that would prepare those chosen for ministry. It was actually a series of classes over a period of three years. The ones called (prophesied over in the prophesy meetings) to any type of ministry were eligible to attend these classes. They still had to be on a special list that the apostle compiled and was revealed every three years after graduation of the previous members.

The fact that Kevin had been called to pastor made us believe that we needed to attend these classes. But you never knew what the apostle was thinking. He had been known to decide in favor of the illogical solution before. It so happened that when the previous class graduated, Kevin and I "were" on that list after we had been there for only three years.

When we began the first year of classes, after a few meetings, the apostle announced that he wanted the students to have mentors. The mentors were comprised of graduates from the class or students who were auditing the class that had already graduated. The mentors were chosen by the apostle specifically for each student.

This process took a couple of weeks. In one of the classes, during this time of appointments, the apostle announced for Kevin and me to meet him in his office. Well, our imaginations were on overdrive. Why was he wanting to talk with us? What had we done? What had we said? Thoughts we would have always steered toward the negative. Different scenarios were being formed in our heads at light speed.

We knocked and stood at the door until he asked us to come in. We went in and sat down quietly in the two chairs that were directly in front of his desk, facing him.

We didn't have to wait long for our fears to be abated.

He looked into our faces and said, "I've called you here because I wanted you to know from me, that I have decided to mentor you, Kevin".

We were speechless and assuredly in shock. After a moment of silence, Kevin recovered and told the apostle how very much he appreciated that decision. There was some small talk afterward and we walked back to class.

We were truly over whelmed. Why us? We never dreamed that we would be mentored directly under the apostle. We were excited, humbled and a little hesitant. But we believed that what he said was truth, so of course we would experience this privilege. We were ready to get started.

Week after week passed. The phone never rang, we were never summoned after the meetings in church or class. We were never addressed in the hallway as he passed. One year folded into the next...and...we never saw the fruition of that commitment come to pass.

We were literally abandoned, left to ourselves to digest what we thought the Lord was teaching us at the time.

The first year of the ministry class continued and was pretty benign. It was mostly about church history, in an elementary sense and how to study the Bible. There was also teaching on how to preach a sermon and how to do a word study among other basic Bible doctrines.

We had to write sermons and submit them. One would be chosen to preach during a Sunday night service. I remember I got my sermon back with White Out all over it. The apostle had written several sentences then used white out to cover what he had said. When I finally made out what some of the words were that had been written for the original grading, by the apostle, I saw that my sermon had been chosen to be preached.

I guess the apostle realized it was mine and being a woman, I was not an acceptable choice. He had also already reined me in once on that Monday morning when we first started coming to the church. He obviously didn't want to allow another opportunity to present itself. I assume he thought I would think I was too big for my britches, again.

The second year took on a more ominous tone. The classes started out with the apostle using these tactics, with a raised voice: humiliation, degradation, discounting, negating, judging and criticizing all of the students. We were told specifically (these sentiments had already been implied from the pulpit) that our feelings, thoughts and opinions were wrong and of no significance. They were dismissed and disregarded.

Does this seem like overkill, using all those verbs? Please believe me when I tell you it's not.

Domination and control continued to be used. Words were spoken to make us feel inferior and our shortcomings were emphasized. He stated in several ways that he was always right and reminded us that we fell short in living the Christian life. We were reminded that we had no control over the major and even minor decisions of our lives. Our hopes, dreams and accomplishments were belittled, and his behavior was contemptuous and disapproving.

Emotional distancing and abandonment ran rampant from the apostle. The first day of class we got the silent treatment and were made to feel we had done something wrong. The whole twenty-three years that we were associated with this place neither the apostle nor his wife

44

ever showed empathy and rarely asked us questions to gather information about ourselves or our well-being.

All these demonstrations of abuse caused those of us who stayed to become passive and compliant. Being from dysfunctional backgrounds certainly didn't help. It just made us want to please them more. Emotional abuse coupled with co-dependent relationships with the apostle and his wife were definitely instrumental in priming us to receive what was dealt out.

We tended to diminish what was happening and make excuses for the way we were treated. We were taught to believe that what we were experiencing was the "baptism of fire" that all Christians, supposedly, had to go through.

Shunning was a common practice, although it was never called that. When a family member left or was kicked out of the church, the rest of the church were not to have anything to do with them. This practice was used to, "bring the person back into the fold by making them realize their sin". Whenever the "apostle" or his wife felt threatened, this form of shunning was used.

The third year is when we moved to start a church in the South and the "on the job training" was considered enough to graduate. We were in the church for a total of five years before we were "sent out" to start a church. When we first moved up north I told Kevin we would only be there for five years. I never dreamed we would leave for this reason.

Our long-term goal had changed. Kevin's career was out the window. Careers were frowned upon. A person had too much autonomy with a career. They were told that they could not serve the Lord effectively when their heart was somewhere else.

I believe this had something to do with the apostle's inferiority complex. He never had a job that would lead to anything and he didn't want anyone else to either. He was a mortician, ran a private nursing home and worked in a parts department for some company.

It was the same with sports. They were frowned upon. He wasn't athletic when he was young so team sports didn't exist in the school.

Careers, education, spouses, where you lived, number of children, how to discipline your children and any other life altering decision was decided by the apostle and his wife. They would even tell you how to dress, what movies you could or couldn't see and even how to wear your make up. Fathers couldn't even dance with their daughters at weddings. When Kevin danced with our daughter at her wedding, it became taboo.

They would manipulate personal situations to coincide with their plans, disregarding what the member wanted. They would accomplish this through directive prophecy, words from the pulpit, direct conversation or use someone in the "leadership" of the church to talk with you. This was all done in the name of the Lord.

Regarding marriage, you were told not to marry anyone outside of the churches that we were associated with. If you did meet someone that was not in the church, they had to go through the Christian education class first and adhere to the apostle's teachings by openly committing themselves to the apostle and the church. If they obeyed, they were usually considered an appropriate candidate for marriage.

The whole congregation was asked to submit their W-2s at the end of each year we were still there. He wanted to make sure that we were tithing ten percent of our *gross* earnings. We were also asked to give above and beyond what we tithed as an offering. When there was a building program everyone was asked to give to the point of sacrifice. We were told we could eat boxed macaroni and cheese for a while if we had to.

Money was crucial for the leadership of this church. They enjoyed very comfortable lifestyles and likely wanted to keep it that way. When the apostle was ready to retire and move to another state, all the churches were required to give one thousand dollars. Not the church as a whole, but each individual family. We had five churches that were associated with the main church at that time. There were anywhere from thirty in the smaller churches to four hundred members in the "home" church. There were no qualms about the "gifts". It was a requirement.

As I'm writing this book, there is a pastor's conference being held and one of the churches that is in another country is being brought back there for the conference. The church is paying for this to be possible, which means the people are paying.

They are asking their people in all four churches to write a card to the apostle and another one for his wife and to put fifty dollars inside of each card. It isn't just the adults that are required to do this but the children, as well, whole families. This totals up to somewhere in the ball park of approximately $30,000.

This is an example of "fleecing the sheep" that occurred regularly.

Benevolence giving was "suggested" to stay within the confines of the churches. We were considered to be the "true" body of Christ – the remnant. To offer assistance to the "nominal" church (people who didn't believe the *whole* gospel) was "casting pearls before swine."

The "whole" gospel, the one that brought eternal life and Jesus as your Savior, had many steps and definitions. There continued to be fences that you had to jump over and as the years went by, the fences increased. There was a complete book written on these steps that the apostle claimed to author. It was used in the Christian education class. We later found out that plagiarism was involved. He had "expanded" on someone else's writings from the church he and his wife had attended before he went into the ministry.

To read the reference about "Latter Rain" in Chapter Three from Kevin's blog is the ideal way to understand these steps. But, I will briefly go through and sum up what would be told to someone who initially wanted to belong to this church.

1.   Repent of your sins and accept the sacrifice of Christ for your justification.

2.   Undergo water baptism in Jesus name for the circumcision of your heart and the remission of your sins. This was representing the new covenant. This event had to take place by someone who had been baptized in the same way.

3.   Receive the Holy Spirit, **for the first time**, (Not at the point of accepting Christ) with evidence of speaking in other tongues.

This doctrine dictates that it's not the blood sacrifice of Jesus that sets you in right relationship with God, it's the water baptism for the circumcision of heart that makes you part of the new covenant.
A fourth step was added before we left to start our own church.

4.   You must be converted.

The apostle and his wife started teaching that we had not been converted as they had been, and we must reach that level of spiritual maturity to be part of the remnant and enter into the "Kingdom".

Basically, being converted meant total surrender to them as the ultimate authority – to see Jesus completely through their eyes. There continued to be levels that must be attained, so you were never spiritual enough to be considered a "son" in the Kingdom of God.

Now it wasn't enough to be born again, part of the remnant, and a son. You had to be converted.

The *real* truth is that the work of Christ accomplishes in us, a completed work, once we believe. Nothing else can be added to or taken away from our state of being translated into His Kingdom of marvelous light. There is nothing that *we* have to do to get there. *He* does it all.

Chapter Six

You're All in or You're All Out

*See to it that no one takes you captive through philosophy
and empty deception, according to the tradition of men,
according to the elementary principles of the world, rather
than according to Christ.*

Colossians 2:8 NKJV

The second year of seminary school began in the fall as usual. Everyone was looking forward to it. All the students were excitedly talking with one another while we were seated in the fellowship hall, waiting for the apostle to come in.

Silence began in the back of the room and quickly moved to the front when "he" entered through the closed doors. He greeted no one and there was an obvious scowl on his face. He looked straight ahead and aimed directly for the front of the room. When he sat in his "teaching" chair, he deliberately looked down at his notes. Silence filled the air for several minutes and the students were frozen, afraid to breathe.

When he finally began to speak, humiliation, degradation, discounting, negating, judging and criticizing all the students were what spilled out of his mouth. We were told specifically (these things had already been implied from the pulpit) that our feelings, thoughts and opinions were wrong and they were dismissed and disregarded.

Domination and control were the underlying intent and were reiterated. Words were used to make us feel inferior and our shortcomings were emphasized. He stated in several ways that he was always right and reminded us that we fell short in living the Christian life. We were reminded that we had no control over the major and even minor decisions of our lives. Our hopes, dreams and accomplishments were belittled, and his behavior was contemptuous and disapproving.

This class was the proof and culmination that emotional distancing and abandonment ran rampant. The first day of class we got the silent treatment and were made to feel we had done something wrong. The whole twenty-three years that we were associated with this place neither the apostle nor his wife ever showed empathy and rarely asked us questions to gather information about ourselves or how we felt.

All these demonstrations of abuse caused those of us who stayed to become passive and compliant. Being from dysfunctional backgrounds certainly didn't help. It just made us want to please them more. We tended to diminish what was happening and make excuses for the way we were treated. We were taught to believe what we were experiencing was the "baptism of fire" that all Christians had to go through.

During the second year of training, Mama and Daddy decided to move up to the church and attend the ministry class with us. Of course, I had given them a gleaming report of how things were going. Never thinking they would actually move up there. They then told me that they wanted to go into ministry with us when it was time.

The apostle was going through a respite of humility. Kevin and I thought that maybe he had seen something, with the help of the Holy Spirit, that was causing a heart-warming. We thought that maybe he was repenting from his domineering ways and becoming more approachable, more loving.

I told Mama about this "new leaf" and before I knew it, they sold their house on the lake and moved into a townhouse not too far from the church. They received directive prophesy from the apostle during a church service and started going to the classes.

If I remember correctly, they were taking the Christian education class at the same time as the seminary class. Mama couldn't handle both, but Daddy tried.

Mama disliked the pastor's/apostle's wife from the very beginning. We went out to dinner one night, all six of us and it was so very awkward. I remember the pastor's wife saying something under her breath after one of Mama's comments. I know Mama heard her. I wanted to slink under the table.

They tried to fit in. They didn't want to disappoint us. Everything was just too obvious to Daddy. He knew what they were teaching was wrong. He could see the manipulation and misuse of authority. And Mama continued to withdraw into her depression more and more.

We were instructed by the apostle to stay the course and not be deceived.

The morning after my parents came to their senses and decided to leave that place was a Sunday. My daddy had a confrontation with the "apostle" a few nights before in our home. He didn't pull any punches. He brought out "the Sword" the word of God and challenged the apostle with what it said. The apostle retreated and said he would not get into a discussion with him.

Even though that was a victory for Daddy, he lost. He lost in the sense that we decided to side with the "apostle". My daddy saw the truth, the unadulterated truth but he couldn't convince us. We were too far gone.

That Sunday morning, during the service, I grieved. I grieved the loss of my parents. I knew shunning was the next step. I cried so hard that I thought I would be sick. Then, suddenly it was like something turned off a faucet. I thought, at the time that it was the Holy Spirit. I thought He had come to give me peace about what had happened.

Looking back, objectively, it was not the Holy Spirit at all. It was a moment of realization. I realized that by us staying, we were pleasing the "man" that had brought us into a truth that supposedly, not many understood. It was a truth that excluded those who didn't receive it and embraced those who accepted the myopic view that only a few would understand. It was a view of the Kingdom of God that wasn't about God at all. It was about power and fear and control. At that point it wasn't about the "truth" it was about the "man".

Compassion? Absent. Grace? Forbidden. Forgiveness? Not likely. This man's approval was all that mattered, even at the cost of my parents.

I have struggled with how I could ever choose this man over my parents. Below, I have written explanations of what happens to those in a cult. The right thing to do is no longer the norm. All logic of descent behavior is turned upside down. Righteousness is redefined.

When you didn't adhere to the teaching of perfect obedience and perfect faith: If you didn't do everything that was asked of you, you would become an apostate - an enemy of the church and in the very end you would either be burning in hell or be dwelling in outer darkness.

You are brainwashed into thinking this is the only way of life to live. Black and white no grey– you live this life, or you have no life. That is why few people leave. We were taught there was nothing else out there. Our total reason for living was within those four walls we called church.

Everyone's choice to decide to be who they aspire to be is taken away. They take away free will. If a young man wanted to grow up to be a doctor, it was discouraged because that profession would take too much time and energy from the Kingdom of God. So, the parents led their child in another direction. Girls were encouraged to stay home and raise a family. They could work at the school that this church had oversight. But, careers were another thing, unless you wanted to be a nurse. The apostle's wife was a nurse.

People who have always wanted to know the truth were particularly drawn to this place. Why are we here? What is our purpose? That is why the directive prophetic meetings were so powerful. In these meetings this question was seemingly answered. Ministries were given out, some high upon the ministerial ladder, others of a humbler nature. In every case, we were only to minister to the people in our church or the churches we were in fellowship with.

When someone new comes in, the appearance of the members is that everything is great. Everyone is smiling and greeting the guest with a hand shake.

I remember my first few communions. We literally broke bread with each other. There was actually a loaf of bread that we passed around, then we would say something like, "Lord bless you" and maybe say a prayer over the person. In the beginning I would be in tears, even sobbing from such an emotional heartwarming biblical event. At that point my relationship with Jesus, my love for Him was intact.

Eventually things changed. I wasn't as touched as I was in the beginning. The Lord's Supper felt like we were just going through the motions as a church. Sometimes, I didn't want to participate. We were taught not to trust our emotions. Crying was frowned upon unless you were responding to the apostle's sermons. I felt numb. I had lost my first Love.

Therefore whoever eats this bread or drinks *this* cup of the Lord in an unworthy manner will be guilty of the body and blood[a] of the Lord. [28]But let a man examine himself, and so let him eat of the bread and drink of the cup. [29]For he who eats and drinks in an unworthy manner[b]eats and drinks judgment to himself, not discerning the Lord's[c] body. [30]For this reason many *are* weak and sick among you, and many sleep. [31]For if we would judge ourselves, we would not be judged.

1 Corinthians 11: 2 NKJV

The Holy Spirit, who had never left me was trying to tell me something. Eventually, I would listen.

If you left, you were told that God's judgment would come back on you double. We were taught to do spiritual warfare against all doubts - to disclaim our own thoughts. We were meant to be God's remnant and that meant guarding against anything with emotion. If you manifested emotions, you weren't in control of your flesh. The remnant was of the spirit and emotions would get in the way and even be your downfall.

Once in seminary school, I remember one of the apostle's sons broke down and started sobbing during an intense session. Instead of the apostle comforting him, the son asked his father to forgive him. He was ashamed of showing such emotion.

Of course, we did have doubts, but we were afraid of those doubts because doubting comes from the "enemy" (the devil). We were taught to say, "What is the truth?" when we practiced "spiritual" warfare. The teaching and grooming we had received from the apostle and his wife were considered the truth. You're all in or you're all out.

Fear was one of the mainstays of this group. It was one of the main weapons that they used for control. If you turned your back on the apostle, you would be turning your back on God and I've made it very clear up to this point what would happen if you did.

This place became our only reality – outside contacts were cut off. There is nothing to compare this experience to because relationships outside the "church" are discouraged and you are told they are wrong. Everything was censored through the apostle's and his wife's personal filters – toys, movies, TV, fashion, music, sports even relationships. Something mentioned from them in idle conversation was elevated to an edict.

You couldn't ask questions. If you made an appointment with the pastor/apostle to talk about concerns or questions, you were marked and watched very closely. They would come up with any wrong doing – even though it really wasn't wrong - to kick you out of the church if they felt challenged.

Family members are asked to sign letters denouncing the family who has been thrown out of the cult. Shunning was practiced throughout the congregation. Members were praised for shunning their families. People would ask, "What was their sin?" trying to understand so they wouldn't make the same mistake. Then **they** would be put on the list.

We thought of leaving, several times. It was just so hard to sever that anchor of allegiance that we had been tied to for so long. And yes, we did worry about our eternal fate. We were taught to not think for ourselves to push any thought away from our mind that was not what the leadership would want. When you stop thinking for yourself it's very easy for someone to control you. The subtle brainwashing of people's minds gets them in a place where they will blindly obey.

Those who leave have a hard time deciding what to eat, what to wear, making any type of decisions for themselves. They go from having every thought under subjection to the apostle to trying to think for themselves.

Many who leave a cult give up their beliefs and try to run away from what they've been through. If they don't seek counseling they may try to ease their pain with alcohol or drugs. They steer clear of churches. They were deceived once, how would they know if they were being deceived again by another tactic?

The leadership never admits to any wrong doing. Since they hear from God, God can never be wrong. They will never admit to making a mistake. They will never ask for an apology, even when they tear people's lives a part. Kevin and I pray for them to repent. We don't know how the Lord will handle all of that, but if they do repent, it will be a miracle. We believe in miracles.

The pain is so intense when you are kicked out that you don't think it will ever go away. You are shunned and ridiculed by people that you loved and looked to as being your family. The ones who leave on their own are no more fortunate, however. They know the consequences and they leave anyway. But the sharp bite of the shunning, the name-calling and the slanderous accusations are felt for years. Eventually, they attempt to move on. We were almost part of that group, enjoying at least the decision to leave rather than the humiliation of being kicked out, but the leaders got to us first. They tore everything that we hold dear away.

God help us.... God help them.

Kevin and I, Kevin especially, have done a lot of research to help us understand how we lost twenty-three years of our lives. Part of that research is demonstrated in the following requirements.

We didn't know what is written below when we were in this *church*. If we had known, it would have saved us a lot pain and heartache.

By reading the requirements below, you will know. You will have a compass and you will not find yourself in a state of loss and despair.

Requirements of an Apostle

The apostle frequently referenced being commissioned by Jesus, Himself, to be an apostle. That is **one** of the major requirements. He allegedly saw Jesus' eyes. We have a dilemma here. Every apostle in the New Testament didn't just see Jesus' eyes. They saw Jesus embodied. They saw the resurrected Jesus, all of Him, physically.

This man self-appointed himself to be called an apostle. There are three **other** requirements to be an apostle, besides seeing the epiphany/physical body of the resurrected Christ:

1. The apostle will suffer. Did this "apostle" suffer? He would tell you that he did. I never saw him go hungry, imprisoned and cold, stoned by an angry mob, almost shipwrecked, blind, suffer from exposure to the elements or living to care for all the churches. When we started our church, we received a phone call every now and then and maybe a visit once a year.

2. The apostle will write an original, foundational word to God's people. That has already been done with the Bible. You cannot add to the existing Word of God. This "apostle" plagiarized the book used in the Christian teaching class and took the already written Word of God and expanded it for the seminary class, along with books from other authors.

For I testify unto every man that heareth the words of the prophecy of this book, if any man shall add unto these things, God shall add unto him the plagues that are written in this book:

Revelation 22:18 NKJV

3. The apostle will produce signs and wonders under the power of the Holy Spirit. With this pastor/apostle, I never saw **one**.

2 Timothy 4:13, 16 – NKJV - [13]Bring the cloak that I left with Carpus at Troas when you come—and the books, especially the parchments. [16]At my first defense no one stood with me, but all forsook me. May it not be charged against them.

Here, Paul the apostle is cold and lonely, he is imprisoned. Yet, he prays for them who deserted him, that they may be delivered from their transgressions.
This is what a "true" apostle does

Testimonial from an Ex –Member # 2

Therefore, what God has joined together, let man not separate.

Mark 10:9 NKJV

*(This account was told to me by the ex-member who didn't feel she could write it herself. These are the events that took place.)

There were many other families who suffered severely under the hand of the leadership. One family in particular, was one of my best friends.

They were a wonderful couple and all the young people and singles loved them dearly. Their daughter had left the church a while back and they were constantly being urged to cut her off. They wouldn't, and this made the now "junior" pastor/apostle, the pastor's son, as well as senior pastor/apostle and wife, furious – strike one.

Meanwhile, their eldest son was newly married to one of the young ladies in the church only a few months before we were kicked out. Please remember that being kicked out is the same as being shunned. No way, no how is anyone from the church allowed to contact us.

My friend and her husband attended a service not long after we were gone. The pastor, two other pastors, all the elders and elders in training called them up to the front of the sanctuary, after the service and started badgering them, in front of the whole church. The spectacle was about them still having contact with us.

The woman calmly said that I was her friend and was ill. (I had been in Kansas City for treatment of Lyme disease). Why wouldn't she talk with me to see how I was doing... because I was shunned. My friend and her husband weren't obeying the commandment of the apostle – strike two.

All of a sudden, the pastor turned the conversation toward their daughter. The pastor asked them directly to cut her off. The man simply said, "I can't do that." This made the pastors furious.

Not only were they fellowshipping their daughter, they also, up to this point, had not put their youngest son back into the school. The church mandated the member's children to go there. They had suspended him for a whole school year for posting something benign on Facebook. My friend had been home schooling him and it was going well. She was glad to keep him away from scrutiny.

For five long months, this couple felt the strain but continued to go through the motions of going to church on Sunday morning and Sunday night, knowing that there was astriction and disfavor from the pastors and the elders.

Finally, the time came where they could go away for a couple of weeks. Before they left, the husband wrote a letter to the pastor telling him that they would not shun their daughter, she was serving the Lord and their son would not be returning to the school.

When they returned from their vacation there was to be a meeting at the church that same night with their close friends and family, including their son and his wife. The meeting was to disparage this couple and undermine relationships in their lives.

Their son already knew about the meeting. He brought their dog home, from keeping her while they were away. When he came in he said to his dad, with tears in his eyes, "I'm going to lose a lot for you and Mom."

They had wondered if the meeting would be about them.

Now it was confirmed from their son's own lips. They had wondered what would happen after they challenged the leadership, the culmination of that decision was about to unfold.

That night, the meeting began, and the pastor did degrade and disgrace this couple. They were put on the reprobate list right up there with us. Both of us would go on to be the main two couples that were a perceived threat to this pastor and church, even to this day. Twenty- three, or so, people left the church that night. The pastor had shown his apocryphal hand and it cost him.

The next day there was a message on their phone. It was from the pastor saying, if they didn't call him and rectify what was in the letter, don't bother coming back. – strike three.

After this happened, their son had to make a decision. After a horrendous time of wrestling with what to do, he made a choice. Although he thought he would be pulled apart by having to choose between not only his parents, but also his siblings and his new wife, he had to choose one. He chose his wife.

One of the pastors told this young man's wife that her husband had no "conviction" that she would have to divorce him.

He went to his dad where he worked. He got on his knees and laid his head in his dad's lap sobbing, "Please make it right Dad. Please make it right." His dad couldn't make it right. The script had been written, the writing was on the wall, all the clichÈs fit. His marriage was over in spite of trying to make the right decision.

Although he made this decision, after he quit his job from his dad's company, turned his truck in and moved from the house that had been provided for him and his wife, the pastor made them separate. They had been married eight months.

That Christmas this young man had to spend it all alone. His wife had separated from him. He couldn't go home to his family, trying to prove his devotion. Not even the church checked on him. He was hanging on to a thread of gossamer. He sent a message to his mom and dad, "I'll be home for Christmas, if only in my dreams."

A month after Christmas they received a phone call from their son. He was hysterical. "She said she's divorcing me and there's nothing I can say to change her mind". My friend simply said, "Come home."

Chapter Seven

New Beginnings

A dark cloud is no sign that the sun has lost its light; and dark black convictions are no arguments that God has laid aside His mercy. [9]

Charles Spurgeon

The fifth year we were in the church (third year of ministry class) is when we moved to start a church in the south. We sold our house there and packed up every last bit of our belongings and stowed them into a moving truck. We stayed with a family in the church that night and I remember looking out the window, in the dark at the truck. It was really happening. It was so strange to know that all of our belongings and our children's belongings...our lives were right there in one small space.

Kevin didn't have a job. We were moving back home in faith. We really wanted to spread what we had learned to the South. There had been directive prophesy, you see. The most significant was from the man that had taught the Christian education class. It went something like this:

His hands laid on Kevin and me "...Sarah! Pack your bags! The Lord has given us a land, a land where we can dig our own wells, not the wells of our fathers..."

Wow! That was significant! I don't know if it was the Lord or if the man had continued to see the spiritual abuse that was going on and he wanted to give us a ticket to freedom. Whatever it was, we knew that the scrutiny that we had undergone for five years was going to soon be far away. We had our ticket home. We were getting out of there.

We moved and rented an apartment in the beginning. Kevin was desperately trying to find a job and door after door kept shutting in his face. School was starting for our children. Our eldest daughter entering eighth grade and our middle daughter going into first, I had no choice but to get a job. Kevin stayed home while I went to work. I had found a job working for a cosmetic company in the large mall there.

One morning, as I was getting ready for work, I found him sobbing uncontrollably in the bathroom. The fact that he had given up everything he had worked for his whole adult life hit him and hit him hard. We had found the panacea of ministry, the ultimate goal for all of life's problems. Yet, here we were, barely rubbing two pennies together and all that Kevin had worked for, a master's degree in economics, working for a nation-wide company with a promising career, had all been tossed aside. He willingly let it all go to "serve the Lord."

I tried to comfort him by talking about the faithfulness of the Lord and how everything would all work out. Yet, all he could see was that he wasn't providing for his family. He saw, as he looked into that bathroom mirror, the personification of a failure. He was searching everywhere for some sort on income. Yet, one of the fast food seafood restaurants wouldn't even hire him to cut fish.

One glorious day, after a couple of months, his old company called him, out of the blue, unexpectedly and asked if he would work on a project for them. Serendipitously, this continued to happen from time to time and we would have enough money to pay the rent in six-month increments. It was like manna from heaven. If nothing else, we knew we had a roof over our heads.

We had a three-year-old son by then, who Kevin stayed at home with while I worked. They would go out in back of the apartment to pick blackberries while the girls were in school, so we could have cobbler for dessert. A little bit of Bisquick and water will perform wonders. Kevin cooked all the meals while I worked full time.

We were on the list with one of the churches in the area to get free food once a month. I would take the children to the thrift store for clothes. The extra discount I received from the department store where I was working came in handy. The Lord provided everything we needed. (We never received a penny from the church up North.)

After a year and a half of Kevin not finding a job, the phone finally rang, and he was hired by a steel company for "IT" work. It didn't pay much, but it was a lot more than what we had been living off of...my measly paycheck and manna. Kevin was thrilled! He was finally supporting his family again.

Around this time, a young couple from the church up north got permission to come down to help us out with starting our church. They ended up staying and the man became Kevin's elder and his closest confidant, beside me.

From the beginning, we had been having church in our home with just our immediate family. When the new family came to join us, we decided it was time to find a storefront to officially open the church doors.

The apostle came down, for one of his rare visits, to sanction a place for us to worship. We made sure that he stayed in the nicest hotel that was closest to our home. Accommodations and meals were all funded by our little church. It was expected.

We showed the apostle three places that we had found. Following his advice, we settled on a space inside a small strip mall, right off one of the major highways. We found a building to rent and began to preach heresy for eighteen years.

Through the years, we went to pastor's conferences that were held in the main church and were treated like royalty. The people were always so glad to see us. And we were glad to see them. I always sensed a silent desperation in the congregation there and in the other churches. Even though I didn't want to admit it, I could relate. We had become part of the elite. We had entered the apostle's circle, so it seemed. But we were still ostracized by the apostle and his wife. We still could never measure up. We were labeled "that little church in the South". And then later – "that little rebel church down there".

This debasement made us want to please them even more. There was a saying that the apostle and his wife quoted a lot, "You become what you behold". Kevin and I wanted to become just like them, I more than Kevin.

I hung on every word that came out of her mouth. She instructed us consistently on how to treat the members of the churches. "You have to be ruthless" she would say. The apostle always agreed.

Through the years, I have wondered just what exactly they meant by that. The actual definition of ruthless is, "Without pity or compassion; cruel; merciless"[10]. What were they trying to achieve by treating people this way?

What did they get out of it? What damage was done in the process?

Now, I look back and am so ashamed of what I became. We taught our people in our church the same elitism that was taught to us; shunning, the existence of sub-normal Christianity, ultimate authority from the pastor, the distorted Gospel, and that we were "the" remnant.

We were aloof in our relationships with our families. We went through the motions of holidays but remained distant. When our families would ask us to come for a celebration, if there was something going on with the church, we would decline. We missed our nieces wedding to attend another pastor's child's wedding. Once Kevin's sister begged him to come over just for a few hours on Christmas day. He adamantly continued to say no. We were emulating the way we had been treated. We were ruthless.

"Just as" (a term used in the Old Testament; Moses built the tabernacle "just as" the Lord God instructed") is another phrase we were taught. We were to follow the apostle's teachings just as they had been delivered. We practiced this complete obedience with the families who attended our church. Although, in the last few years we began to turn away from this legalistic, judgmental approach, the damage had been done.

Ironically, exhibiting more grace toward our people and our families cost us everything. We were in direct opposition to the apostle and his wife. As far as they were concerned we were in rebellion. They did not like the example we were sending forth and they were determined to make us pay.

We would have visitors come to see what God had

to offer in our little church but very few came back. We were small, only a few families. We went from the store front to a log cabin that had been some sort of shop at one time. There was no way we could afford the rent, but the landlord made it work. A Church of Christ was used to hold baptisms. We had fellowship meals in our homes. We would take turns. Through it all, the church was very close. Kevin and I were especially close to our children.

Our children went to private Christian schools. We were always careful to learn what the school's mission statement was, so we could tell our children which beliefs were according to what we believed and which ones weren't.

We allowed friendships with the other children in these Christian schools but were careful. Our eldest daughter met her future husband at school. Of course, he had to come to the church and follow the Gospel accordingly, being baptized in Jesus name for the circumcision of his heart and remission of sins and receive the Holy Spirit with evidence of speaking in tongues. He also had to attend the nine-month Christian education class. He graduated and then pledged his allegiance to our church.

My eldest daughter graduated from the Christian school she attended. She got a scholarship to become a nurse at the community college. When she got married she quit nursing, after she had their son, our grandson, to stay at home and focus on being a wife and mother.

I started home schooling my younger daughter when she was beginning eighth grade and my youngest, our son, when he was starting third grade. They both graduated with scholarships. Kevin coached girl's and boys' basketball teams as well as track for the home school we were affiliated with. We played against other Christian schools throughout the area. Our son and daughter participated. Our daughter was also a cheerleader. Sports was something that the apostle disapproved of. We were over seven hundred miles away from the watchful eyes of the leadership in the church up North. We remained in the "log cabin" for many years. A couple started coming to the church and decided they felt safe enough to stay. They had been through a roller coaster of pseudo Christianity and felt that they could put down some roots in our church.

After they had been there a while, the woman's employer started to visit with her. The woman did housework for this visitor and they had become friends. The employer happened to be going through a divorce from a very wealthy man at the time. When she finally got her settlement, after a long and drawn out court battle, she tithed from what she received. Over a period of time she gave a significant amount of money to our little church.

We had saved an additional amount of money from our tithes. With the coffers full, we started looking for land all over the city. My daughter married the young man who had joined the church. His family lived in a rural area where land was a little less expensive. We prayed, and land became available for the amount we could afford. We bought 3 acres. We were on our way to constructing our very own church building.

My daughter and her husband went before us and built a house very close to the church property. They wanted to set an anchor for what we were embarking on. We were going to have to build the building ourselves. We all pitched in, the whole church. We worked every single moment that wasn't designated to our jobs, school or sleep. Even sleep gave up many hours for what we felt the Lord was having us do.

There were five men and two teenage boys doing the majority of the work. The women would cook meals and take them down to the property for the men. We women also worked on the church when it was needed. Once, we all worked way into the night laying rebar for the slab that was to be poured the next day. We had a deadline. The cement truck was coming early the next morning.

We were one big family. We all pitched in for whatever was needed. We had fun too. We would get together for movie nights or to play games. We worked together, ate together and played together. But there were no new faces who joined us in our endeavor.

We continued to have church in Kevin's and my daylight basement. We moved out near the property, as well. Soon the elder and his family moved nearby. His mother was living with him at the time. We were all from the main church and the elder's family had a very long, committed history there.

Kevin and I wondered why the Lord was blessing us monetarily but not with people. Looking back, it all makes perfect sense. Not only did the Lord not want more of His children subjected to heretical teaching, there was something else - something that we never could have even imagined back then.

It took us five years to finish the building. We did everything from digging the foundation and filling sink holes to setting the trusses. The only thing we didn't do was put the brick on the outside of the building.

Within those five years, young men from the other churches would make long trips down to help. There would be times that we would have at least six or seven at once. They loved coming and we loved having them. Kevin would barbeque, or I would make huge pots of chili. The other families pitched in too.

When the day was done we would all get together at my daughter's and son–in–law's for games, food and fellowship. We would laugh until our stomachs ached. Being with us, so far away from their home churches, was a reprieve for these young men. Everyone sensed that this new building meant something and they all felt privileged to be a part of it.

Unfortunately, these precious young men were so excited about the building and Kevin's preaching, they would go back home and tell their pastors all about it. One pastor, in particularly, was livid about the news. (The apostle had "retired" by this time and his son was the pastor now and apostle by "proxy". The Lord never intended for the office of apostle to be handed down by birth right.) These young men would ask why *he* – the apostle's son - didn't preach what Kevin preached. Or, they would tell him about Kevin swinging from the trusses with a nail gun.

Finally, this pastor and his wife decided to come down for a few days for a visit. They had talked with us about helping out with the building. Bring your overalls, I teased. You're going to need them.

It was almost time for them to leave and they still hadn't set foot inside the building. One morning I saw their car coming down the graveled driveway toward the church. He got out while she stayed seated in the car.

He called Kevin aside and had a talk with him. It was Sunday and every Sunday for the past four years we would all go to church in our basement, have a large fellowship meal upstairs after, then the men would go to the property to work.

This pastor, the apostle's son, had called his mom and dad and "tattled" on us. Our harborage of freedom had been interrupted and everything that we had considered "right" was "wrong". He proceeded to tell Kevin that he really shouldn't ask the men to work on Sunday. Sunday was a day of rest and his mom and dad said so.

Building a habitation for the Lord's people and the Lord as well, was not important enough to get finished. Were we pushing these men? Yes. Were we focusing on getting this church built instead of other things? Yes. The men were working during the week at their "day" jobs and the weekends were all we had. Kevin would go down to do what he could every night when he got home from work.

In this same conversation that was taking place, the pastor from the main church actually said that the young men who came down looked at Kevin as Superman. The pastor said "he" couldn't swing from the trusses like Kevin. What was he to do?

It began. From that point on that pastor and his parents, who were already continually looking for problems, began to put consequences to what they saw. And if they couldn't find anything wrong, they would look for someone who could. That pastor nor his wife ever set foot in the church we were building during the four days they were there.

Chapter Eight

Law vs Spirit

[5] "Not that we are sufficient of ourselves to think of anything as being from ourselves, but our sufficiency is from God, [6]who also made us sufficient as ministers of the new covenant, not of the letter but of the Spirit; for the letter kills, but the Spirit gives life.

NKJV II Corinthians 3:5-6

There were a few times when the apostle's wife would invite me to lunch. We would be having a nice conversation, then, she would change the tone of her voice and begin belittling me and telling me things that I was doing wrong. She always wanted to know if I was shunning my family. She would tell me stories about how she shunned hers to try and convince me to do likewise.

Kevin and I knew we were being disobedient, but we just couldn't cut our families off completely. Little did we realize at the time, that the leadership of the church, those in charge, were actually keeping records of our behavior. Later we learned that they had a file on everyone in the church. They told us themselves.

Once she invited me to lunch and gave me a beautiful book of poetry. We were sitting there having a lovely time when her whole mood changed. She began admonishing me for being too involved in our church back home. I was supposed to emulate her, and I was too involved? What a dichotomy!

I had too much input in the decision making. I gave

Kevin too much advice. I was involved with too much counseling. Kevin and I looked at ourselves as a team. I certainly wasn't stepping on *his* toes.

By the end of our lunch date, I felt like I had been wrung out and hung up to dry. That beautiful book that she had so ardently given me was tainted. That is a perfect analogy of what happened to all my hopes and dreams and twenty-three years of my life. They were tainted and dismissed by the hands of the apostle and his wife.

At one time, there was a church out of the country and the apostle and his wife were living with the pastor and his family there for a period of time. The apostle had some *mentoring* to do with this pastor and his wife.

It was a beautiful place to live, although the crime, Voodoo and drug abuse were off the charts. As long as you stayed in the resorts, you were fine. The pastor lived outside of that safety zone. Yet, we were invited to visit - so we did.

There was one day when the apostle's wife and I hung out and did some shopping. We went into a gift shop and she offered to buy me something. She asked me to pick it out. I was overwhelmed with her generosity and I little shy about picking something out. I began looking around the shop trying to find something that wasn't too expense and something that would fit into my suitcase.

After a while she said that we were leaving. She opened the screen door and we walked out. She never spoke about the gift or that I took too long or kiss my conch shell! All I could process in my brain was that expectations had not been met. I had failed. I wasn't fast enough. I had not met the requirement for picking out gifts. My status in the

Kingdom of God had plunged. I just wanted to go home.

Neither Kevin nor I were ever thanked or encouraged that we were doing a good job or that we were successfully being "obedient" by her. It was always negative, demeaning feedback. We never rose to her expectations. Having a conversation with her was like walking through an area of land mines.

The apostle was more gracious than she was, but all his compliments had a condition to them. He would thank us for a service that we extended to him. Then, there was a follow up. If you had only done it "this way" it would have been better.

The apostle's wife began to wield as much power as the apostle did and eventually more. The apostle was taking pain pills, narcotics, I don't know how many or the different types. He would always tell us and the congregation that he was taking a lot. He eventually began using a wheelchair. I don't know if he was trying to take on the role of a martyr or if he truly needed it. Maybe he thought people having sympathy for him would make him more credible. As I stated before, his wife was a nurse. She knew the ramifications of all the drugs. She began to treat him as an invalid... he started believing it.

As hard as we tried to please them, it was never enough. The tragic part of never measuring up is it caused constant self-doubt, even self- loathing. As I mentioned before, we were constantly told to do "just as". This little phrase became a mantra for the church. Kevin and I didn't do "just as". We were rebellious, and rebellion is as witchcraft. So, ultimately this was our downfall. The love of Jesus Christ was replaced with accolades for doing "just as".

15 "Beware of false prophets, who come to you in sheep's clothing, but inwardly they are ravenous wolves.
16 You will know them by their fruits. Do men gather grapes from thornbushes or figs from thistles?
17 Even so, every good tree bears good fruit, but a bad tree bears bad fruit.
18 A good tree cannot bear bad fruit, nor can a bad tree bear good fruit.
19 Every tree that does not bear good fruit is cut down and thrown into the fire.
20 Therefore by their fruits you will know them.

NKJV Matthew 7: 15-20

The Lord is very specific about what happens to the shepherds that put themselves before the sheep. This was the norm in the behavior of the apostle, his wife and their son.

In Chapter Four, I mention many examples of how the apostle fleeced the sheep monetarily on a regular basis; when there were building funds to be raised, or traveling expenses, even birthdays, the sheep had to cough up the funds to satisfy the expense.

But also, illness in that church was an inconvenience. The weak were frowned upon, accused of being disobedient which caused their problems. Past abuses from outside the church were ignored. The emotionally injured were a burden.

Sheep took care of sheep. All the above ministry was passed off to the congregation.

The strays and lost weren't only treated as being dead. Many times, it was much worse. They were treated as if they never existed.

Therefore, these ex members were ignored, left without a compass. They were left for the world to destroy and many fell in pits of apathy and self- destruction.

The following scripture says it all.

The LORD Will Be Israel's Shepherd – Ezekiel 34 NKJV

1 And the word of the Lord came to me, saying,

2 "Son of man, prophesy against the shepherds of Israel, prophesy and say to them, 'Thus says the Lord God to the shepherds: "Woe to the shepherds of Israel who feed themselves! Should not the shepherds feed the flocks?

3 You eat the fat and clothe yourselves with the wool; you slaughter the fatlings, but you do not feed the flock.

4 The weak you have not strengthened, nor have you healed those who were sick, nor bound up the broken, nor brought back what was driven away, nor sought what was lost; but with force and cruelty you have ruled them.

5 So they were scattered because there was no shepherd; and they became food for all the beasts of the field when they were scattered.

6 My sheep wandered through all the mountains, and on every high hill; yes, My flock was scattered over the whole face of the earth, and no one was seeking or searching for them."

7 'Therefore, you shepherds, hear the word of the Lord:

8 "as I live," says the Lord God, "surely because My flock became a prey, and My flock became food for every beast of the field, because there was no shepherd, nor did My shepherds search for My flock, but the shepherds fed themselves and did not feed My flock"--

9 therefore, O shepherds, hear the word of the Lord!

10 Thus says the Lord God: "Behold, I am against the shepherds, and I will require My flock at their hand; I will cause them to cease feeding the sheep, and the shepherds shall feed themselves no more; for I will deliver My flock from their mouths, that they may no longer be food for them."

11 'For thus says the Lord God: "Indeed I Myself will search for My sheep and seek them out.

12 As a shepherd seeks out his flock on the day he is among his scattered sheep, so will I seek out My sheep and deliver them from all the places where they were scattered on a cloudy and dark day.

13 And I will bring them out from the peoples and gather them from the countries and will bring them to their own land; I will feed them on the mountains of Israel, in the valleys and in all the inhabited places of the country.

14 I will feed them in good pasture, and their fold shall be on the high mountains of Israel. There they shall lie down in a good fold and feed in rich pasture on the mountains of Israel.

15 I will feed My flock, and I will make them lie down," says the Lord God.

16 I will seek what was lost and bring back what was driven away, bind up the broken and strengthen what was sick; but I will destroy the fat and the strong, and feed them in judgment."

17 'And as for you, O My flock, thus says the Lord God: "Behold, I shall judge between sheep and sheep, between rams and goats.

When we were pastoring our church, before the building was finished, there were scales on our eyes and we couldn't see what we had become. I went from being an easy going, non- judgmental, accepting person (with the gift of mercy) to...well, being just like them. Twenty years of becoming what I was beholding was evident. I was constantly "critiquing" the way Kevin did things. He didn't preach the way he should, take care of the church business in the right way, talk to people correctly. I judged people severely. I had a lofty image of myself that created a distance between our congregation and me.

Kevin, on the other hand, became passive. The intimidation and constant reiteration of not measuring up caused him to emotionally – shut down. He wanted to please this man who he believed was the mouth piece of God. The co-dependency that was way too familiar, was raring it's crippled head.

We never sensed any conviction from the Holy Spirit. The sense of biblical spiritual rights and wrongs had been stifled. Now what was right and wrong was twisted and myopic. Our need for their acceptance replaced any principle that we once owned as truth. We had no ambition or view for our future that didn't line up to their expectations. As long as we pleased "the man" there was no feeling of guilt, no feeling of being off base, because, we were doing just as we were told.

Once we were going to dinner with the apostle and his wife. She and I were in the back seat and she started talking about her mother and how she finally decided enough was enough. She went to see her mother in the hospital. Her mother said something she didn't like and she, then and there, cut her off. She never saw her again.

In that same conversation, she talked about going to a family funeral. She knew she would see this particular cousin that she didn't like. Her narrative turned in the direction of how good she looked at that funeral. She had on her mink coat and was dressed to the nines. Her jewelry was sparkling, and that cousin was dumbfounded. The apostle was nodding to every word.

Why did I share this with you? Because this is the epitome of where their heart was...themselves. I believe there had been a time when they truly cared for the hungry, the sick, the poor. Yet, even now they only care about their comfort and they're not embarrassed to ask their people in the churches to fund it for them.

The following scripture is very specific about how the Lord feels about this.

18 Is it too little for you to have eaten up the good pasture, that you must tread down with your feet the residue of your pasture--and to have drunk of the clear waters, that you must foul the residue with your feet?
19 And as for My flock, they eat what you have trampled with your feet, and they drink what you have fouled with your feet."

Ezekiel 34 NKJV

I firmly believe the apostle doesn't care if he takes your best and leaves you with the rest. He doesn't care if he takes your children's college fund, your retirement or even your house payment for the month. *They* deserve your sacrifice.

When the church we were building was finished, the scales started falling away from our eyes. It was a slow and arduous process. After all we had given to this man and his wife, it was very hard to let our allegiance go. We remembered the prophesy that our teacher of the Christian education class had spoken to us.

"You will dig your own wells and not the wells of your fathers." We started out with small situations, not even realizing it. We began following less and less the edict of the apostle.

Most of our women didn't wear stockings to church as required by the apostle's wife. The heat index in the summer could get well beyond one hundred degrees in the deep south.

Our children participated in sports and cheerleading. As I mentioned before, Kevin even coached basketball and track. We were writing our own praise and worship songs. We told people about Jesus and what He did for us on the cross without getting into the rest of the "gospel" that we had learned in the Christian education class. AND...we had worked on the building after church on Sundays.

What did Jesus do on the Sabbath?

1 At that time Jesus went through the grainfields on the Sabbath. And His disciples were hungry and began to pluck heads of grain and to eat.

2 And when the Pharisees saw it, they said to Him, "Look, Your disciples are doing what is not lawful to do on the Sabbath!"

3 But He said to them, "Have you not read what David did when he was hungry, he and those who were with him:

4 how he entered the house of God and ate the showbread which was not lawful for him to eat, nor for those who were with him, but only for the priests?

5 Or have you not read in the law that on the Sabbath the priests in the temple profane the Sabbath, and are blameless?

6 Yet I say to you that in this place there is One greater than the temple.

7 But if you had known what this means, 'I desire mercy and not sacrifice,' you would not have condemned the guiltless.

8 For the Son of Man is Lord even of the Sabbath."

NKJV   Matthew 12: 1 - 8

Jesus also healed on the Sabbath; Matthew 12: 9 – 14 NKJV

There are more examples of the apostle and his wife living by the letter of the Law and not the Spirit. They still live under the Old Covenant in many aspects; living by the literal letter, not what the Spirit is conveying, praise and worship, water baptism, dealing with their people harshly with the threat of punishment, expecting their people to obey them "just as" they commanded.

I remember the apostle's wife held a meeting once to demonstrate how to die to your convictions and emotions. "You must be as a dead man", she said. "Dead men don't feel you sticking them with a pin. When you receive instruction and teaching just be as a dead man and obey". Paul teaches us the difference and consequence of the Law and the Spirit – This scripture is in contrast to the perspective of the apostle's wife.

6 who also made us sufficient as ministers of the new covenant, not of the letter but of the Spirit; for **the letter kills**, but the **Spirit gives life.**

II Corinthians 3:6 NKLV

Testimonial of an Ex-Member # 3

The beginning of the end started approximately in 1988 when my wife and I met with the senior pastor/apostle to talk about why he was asking people to go into personal debt in order for the church to build the new sanctuary. My wife and I gave the church $25,000.00 and I felt strongly that there were prophesies from a guy who was a prophet that the "apostle" trusted, that clearly spoke to the leadership not to require people to go into debt to build the church, that God would provide from those who could afford to give. So we humbly and respectfully questioned the senior pastor and the response we got was that it was none of our business.

After that meeting things changed. I felt that the senior pastor was always trying to find fault with me. He made it very difficult for me to function. In 1989 he found out that I was talking negatively about the church with a friend. He and I would often meet forbreakfast.I remember one morning I said to him that something was wrong with the church and that it was not normal that we were being isolated from other churches and our families. Months later this conversation made it back to the pastor. Late spring early summer of 1989 at a Sunday morning service, he called me out in front of the whole congregation and accused me of causing my friend to stumble and lose the kingdom. I had to meet him (the pastor/apostle) and his wife with all the Elders present. It was a Tuesday evening. I remember because the choir was rehearsing.

My wife was present also. We came in separate vehicles because I was not allowed in my home. The pastor had told her to separate from me. I was staying in a motel. I was extremely traumatized from what had happened the previous Sunday.

At this meeting (the pastor/apostle) questioned me about what I said to my friend. While my wife was sitting there he and his wife asked me if I was ever unfaithful to my wife. I said no! So, they dug deeper asking if I ever touched another woman or kissed another woman. I said no! So, then the pastor accused me of emotionally abusing my wife and felt that she could divorce me based on that.

Then He read scripture to me about if you cause someone to stumble it would be better to drown in the ocean with a millstone around my neck. I believed everything he said and agreed with him that I had committed a horrible sin by talking to my friend.

I agreed to live with a family in the church who lived nearby for a month. During that month I was instructed not to have any contact with my wife and the children. I complied except for one night I missed the kids so much I drove to the house. The kids were happy to see me. My oldest daughter freaked out and told me I was not to be there. My other daughter said my dad can be here anytime he wants because he is my Dad! I'll never forget that.

That was a very hard summer. In August of 1989 the assistant pastor was giving marriage counseling to my wife and me. Everything we talked about was written in a report and given to the pastor/apostle. In September my wife and I went on a vacation to reconcile. After we got back I moved back home. Like I said I did everything I was told to do.

Now for the next 3 months everything was back to normal except I was not allowed to sing in the choir. The pastor told me I could never be involved with any type of ministry in the church. Forever!! I was fine with that. I was just happy to be back with my family.

But the pastor was not satisfied with all that! They started to attack my son in school. They wanted us to spank him more, so he would do better in school. They used the words box him in. My wife and I resisted and decided that they had gone too far by attacking our children. So, we took him out of the school. We put him in a different Christian school.

Then we were back in the pastor's office with his wife and all the Elders. We were told that my son would not ever be allowed to play with any of the kids at that church. We left that meeting totally confused and full of fear. My wife and I decided to call a pastor that my brother suggested we talk to about what we were going through. So that Sunday in late December 1989. We visited this pastor's church.

At that service the Pastor prayed for us and asked for everyone in the church to kneel down and pray for my wife and me and our kids. The Holy Spirit delivered us that night.

The next morning, I called the school and told them that our children would no longer be attending. The pastor/apostle called me and said some nice things and happy memories and wished us good luck. He also suggested that we move out of the area and look for a new job, since I was employed by a man in the church. He also told me to write a letter of resignation from the church, even though I was not in any kind of leadership position. I wrote it.

Many other things transpired as we were trying to adjust to our new life outside of that church

Chapter Nine

Punished Expectations

Do not quench the Spirit -I Thessalonians 5:19 NKJV

Dedication of our building to the Lord was a significant event. We had looked forward to this day from the time we broke ground for the building. What a time of celebration it would be! We would dance before the Lord, praising Him for His faithfulness. We would sing to him and be glad!

Kevin and I started planning for this glorious day. We wanted special music that our daughter and son in law would perform, along with their best friends from the main church. We planned the order of the service and the menu for the luncheon afterward. This was to be the exclamation point on five years of back breaking labor.

Kevin and I were very good friends with a pastor and his wife from another church in the city where we lived. She had the voice of an angel. We asked her if she would honor us by singing at the dedication. She graciously agreed, and we were thrilled.

Although the pastor wanted a list of the songs we had chosen to be sung, and what was on the menu for the luncheon, there wasn't much else he had control over.

We basically planned the whole thing ourselves without much input from up north and that wasn't received very well. This was proven with the beginning of the service. When the service started the atmosphere in that place was as cold as ice. No one was clapping to the music. No one stood up. I was sitting next to my best friend at the time, who was a pastor's wife from another church in the association. Her hands were folded in her lap. I looked at her in total disbelief.

I went to the middle of the aisle and started dancing. Nothing. Everyone sat still right where they were. No "praise you Lords," or "thank you Jesus'" came from any of the congregants. I looked around the sanctuary. I paused for a few seconds on the faces that I recognized as being one who I would call friend. They looked back. Some expressions were those of embarrassment. Others were stone cold.

Definition of a Friend: one attached to another by affection or esteem - one that is not hostile - *Is he a friend or an enemy?*

Merriam-Webster

What a conundrum – how could those people who were attached to me by affection and esteem - be my enemies?

1 John 3: 14 We know that we have passed from death to life, because we love the brethren. He who does not love his brother abides in death.

15 Whoever hates his brother is a murderer, and you know that no murderer has eternal life abiding in him.

16 By this we know love, because He laid down His life for us. And we also ought to lay down our lives for the brethren.

17 But whoever has this world's goods, and sees his brother in need, and shuts up his heart from him, how does the love of God abide in him?

NKJV

Merriam-Webster and John the Apostle form a dichotomy with the moral compass of all the people who attend the main church and the few smaller churches. As long as you listen to the apostle and his wife and do as they say, friendship is viable. But! If you decide to leave or are asked to leave (kicked out) hostility rises up and overcomes everything that you and that friend built together.

Affection, love, esteem is turned off like a faucet. The behavior of people who belong to a cult is fascinating. I look at my own behavior, when I was there and compare it to now. What is the determining factor that causes such a radical change? John sheds the light of truth in the following:

1 John Chapter 3
14 We know that we have passed from death to life, because we love the brethren. He who does not love his brother abides in death.
15 Whoever hates his brother is a murderer, and you know that no murderer has eternal life abiding in him.
16 By this we know love, because He laid down His life for us. And we also ought to lay down our lives for the brethren. NKJV

The apostle and his wife often said, "You become what you behold". There is a transference that takes place with the apostle and the Lord. Maybe at one time you had a vibrant relationship with the Lord. His presence in your life was clear and bright. When you became part of a cult the shadow of the one in charge moves as a dark cloud to hide the truth of who God really is.

How in the world can you see God and receive His love? How can you in turn love others when the apostle is blocking your view? You can't. You don't. You become what you are beholding, the apostle and his wife.

When people ask me how I could have gotten mixed up with something like this cult, I try to explain the best I can, but my explanations don't connect with logic. It's not logical. It's spiritual. Every cult has the same spirit. Although some of the practices are different, the underlying paradigm is the same.

The group of people that came to our Dedication were being controlled. They were being controlled by the apostle and his wife. The element that was used was fear – fear of Hell, fear of not being good enough – acceptable, fear of missing the Kingdom of God.

Whatever preconceived idea that these "friends" had of the Lord's love and His truth had been washed away. It was replaced with the dictates of a man's interpretations.

Many of the people's biggest fear was disappointing the apostle. Nothing, nothing, nothing was more important than that. Codependent behavior was looked upon as being normal. It was even celebrated.

So, you see, the edict had been announced to everyone to not participate at the Dedication. Friendship didn't stand a chance against being found unworthy by the ultimate authority.

Five years of anticipation, looking forward to that day was stolen. We were robbed of our joy and thanksgiving to the Lord for His faithfulness. We hadn't been obedient to the authority and we were being punished for it.

The people had been told not to participate. Our "friends"

had been told not to participate. Our poor daughter and the others on stage could see everyone's faces and they just had to keep singing and playing. They had to keep going.

Lord knows what my poor friend, who we invited to sing, thought as she used her beautiful voice as a love offering unto the Lord and she saw those cold eyes staring back at her. If I had known, even suspected, I would have warned her. It seems I still had a little bit of civility in my heart.

When the apostle's son got up to preach, his expression was solemn, even severe. He said from the pulpit that the Lord had given us this beautiful new building, but to be careful. Obey the Lord/apostle (the two were the same to him) so that it doesn't get taken away. This was an omen, a warning of things to come.

We had a luncheon prepared afterward to feed our guests and of course we asked our pastor friends to sit at the pastor's table with us. I was so embarrassed. Hardly anyone would speak to them.

I want to think that the fact they were African American had nothing to do with the way they were received. I don't know about that. Maybe inviting them was just one more step toward our demise, representing our rebellion to the apostle and his wife.

Of course, that is the filter the leadership of the main church was seeing our decision through. Yet, they were missing the mark by a mile. We didn't invite them because we were being rebellious! We invited them because we loved them and wanted to share this monumental occasion with them.

We had been in the same home school group together. Their two sons played basketball for the school. Kevin was coaching both the girl and boy teams. One night after a game, we all went to a restaurant. I sat at the same table with this lovely woman and we just...connected. We never looked back.

No, they didn't go to any of the churches we were in association with. In fact, her husband was a pastor of a church on the other side of town. However, I saw more of Jesus in those two than in all the leadership of all the churches put together.

When everything fell apart, we showed up at their home unannounced. They opened their door to us and cooked us dinner. They were there, tangibly there, a respite of normal in the midst of antipathy.

There was a young man who was dear to our hearts and a wonderful photographer. He was from the northern church but had been very instrumental in helping us build "our" church as a lot of men and young men from the other churches had been.

We asked him to take pictures of the sequence of events as they happened that Sunday. The events that we had hoped and planned for during the past five years. He was more than willing, and we were very grateful.

Later we found out that the pictures that this young man took suspiciously had been stolen. On his way home, he said that his camera was stolen from the backseat of his car because he forgot to lock it. So...we had no memories to look back on, nothing to tangibly hold in our hands from that day.

We began to take "baby steps" in following what we believed Jesus, our Lord was saying to us. We were soon labeled, "That rebellious little church down there in the South," spoken acerbically by the apostle's wife herself.

To illustrate how the apostle's wife started to gain so much momentum, regarding her authority, I've written the following event.

Once, when the apostle's wife came for a visit, we went to a mall in our area and spent the day.

We came upon a pretzel shop and decided to rest for a bit and have a snack. We talked small talk for a few minutes then she told me something that I still marvel about.

She said she knew that there was not a precedent in the Word about women being apostles or having a ministry equal to an apostle. However, she said, the Lord spoke directly to her one night when she was in bed and told her that she was different. It was some type of reward for being faithful.

I believe I was being given this information to let me know "she" already had a plan to turn our church on its ear. She and the apostle always told us that what they say in conversation is never idle talk. It's always for a reason. I believe there was a web of destruction being spun and we were to be the prey. She was adding to the Bible – the Word of God - and telling me that "she" was chosen to fulfill a ministry that would turn the world upside down.

The apostle had not been doing well physically for quite a long while at this point. She was beginning to not just handle the women in the churches but the men too. Even at the weekend long Pastor's Meetings she began to sit up front by the apostle. To Kevin's and another pastor's detriment, the time would come when she would sit in the front of the room, without the apostle, alone.

She is now in her little corner of the world and has, I think, way too much time on her hands. She dictates over the people that she has left, and the number is getting smaller by the year. When we started to not adhere to her words or the apostle's words, for that matter, we were labeled sinners - worse than sinners, really. We were depraved. We were the ones who would dwell in outer darkness. There was no recourse or forgiveness, as far as they were concerned. To continue to disobey (hear from the Lord yourself) meant reprobation, especially because Kevin was a pastor.

13Then the king said to the servants, 'Bind him hand and foot, and throw him into the outer darkness; in that place there will be weeping and gnashing of teeth.' 14For many are [a]called, but few are chosen.

Matthew 22: 13-14 NKJV

Our obedience to the apostle determined if we were chosen, if we belonged to the remnant.

There were spies within our church who fed information back to the leadership. There was a family who had been with us from the beginning. When everything fell apart it was the man's mother who had come down to "help support us" who was one of the spies. The other was a single woman who came from one of the churches that had been shut down. One of these ladies or maybe both, told the apostle that we were evangelizing.

Isn't that sad? We were telling people about Jesus and were called out for it.

These ladies were chosen to look for problems. We were constantly in survival mode – when we would receive CDs of the apostle giving instruction or congregational letters, we were careful not to show emotion if we disagreed with what was being asked of us.

One thing we were learning, by being a part of this cult for twenty-three years, is what Martin Luther said when *he* realized that you don't need a man to dictate your moral precedent... ""Jesus is enough".

After the Dedication, we settled into a normal routine of services on Sunday morning, Sunday night and Wednesday night. But we could feel stirrings in the air. They were faint at first, like the gentle lapping of waves on the sand at low tide. Somehow, we knew the tranquility wouldn't last long. We knew we would be heading into some rough water. Yet, we never dreamed we would ultimately find ourselves under the deafening roar of a tidal wave.

Chapter Ten

Sheep in Wolves Clothing

Beware of false prophets that come to you in sheep's clothing but inwardly they are ravenous wolves.
Matthew 7:15 NKJV

I had finally been diagnosed with Lyme Disease around 2006. I say finally because I was bitten in 1979 on a canoe trip before Lyme was even discovered. I had a series of unexplained illnesses through the years. When I finally saw a picture of the "bull's eye" rash that the tick leaves behind, I knew.

I am a registered nurse and didn't want to believe it was Lyme because many doctors believed humans couldn't contract the disease. But it was Lyme and my next challenge was finding someone who would treat me. We started going to another state, to a clinic, for treatment because where we were living wouldn't acknowledge that systemic Lyme Disease existed. Therefore, I couldn't receive medical help at home. Eventually I ended up in a wheelchair.

We went to this clinic once a month and developed an affinity for the area we visited. Before we knew it, we had started a Bible study there. We knew this had to be discussed with the apostle. It just all happened so fast. People were hungry for the Word of God.

Kevin went to a wedding at the main church and the apostle's wife cornered him. "What's this I hear about you starting a church in ***** ********?", she asked. News had gotten back to her from a dear friend that I entrusted our thoughts and plans to. I didn't see anything wrong. Weren't we supposed to spread the Good News?

Kevin tried to explain to her that we weren't starting a church. He had already spoken to the apostle about the Bible study. We had every intention of letting the apostle know the details as they unfolded.

Kevin knelt beside her chair, took her hand and impeached her to believe him. "You would know before anything like that would ever happen." He said.

"You just go and pastor that little rebel church of yours down there in the South", she said. "You don't need to worry about a Bible study.'

This was quite a dilemma. We believed the Lord Himself was leading us and had hoped that the apostle would understand. We believed, at the time, one of the young men in our church was meant to take over the Bible Study and eventually pastor a church there.

We never found out if it was truly the Lord or not. *Man* took over. We would have been teaching heresy anyway... unless, the Lord allowed the scales to fall away from our eyes. We still wonder to this day

Later that year, some of our members were graduating from the ministry school that Kevin was teaching, he was trying to emulate the apostle's authority, as far as the classes were concerned. We thought someone from one of the churches should come down to share in our celebration. This was the protocol when the other churches had graduations. We were thinking of the couples who were graduating. They had put three years of hard work into this class.

Well, we certainly got what we asked for and more.

The apostle's wife and their son, who was now the pastor/apostle of the church up there, came down for the graduation service. We were thankful that someone had come to *support* us during this special time.

We put them up in one of the best hotels in town, took them to the best restaurants and our congregation was there for their every whim. In other words, we did exactly what we had been taught to do. We were a very small church to put out such a large red carpet. It was all taken for granted.

We were being set up. The fact that *she* came should have been a red flag. There was always an ulterior motive when it came to her presence. Instead of receiving support, we had stirred up a hornet's nest.

Sunday morning arrived, and we were all expectant. She nonchalantly asked questions while we were giving her a tour of the church. She asked about our son in law who was one of the graduates. She wanted to know what his plans were. They were basically what the apostle had told him they would be years before. The apostle had essentially told him, prophetically, that he and Kevin would minister hand in hand. He would take over the church as pastor and Kevin would move on to what the Lord had called him to do.

As we were walking and talking, something we said hit a nerve. She had an agenda and used what we said to confirm it. She twisted our words to accommodate her plans.

It was time for the service to begin. She walked up to the pulpit, with help, and began her attack. She talked about how our association of churches were the only ones with the truth. She said we were the remnant. She then pointed her metaphorical finger at Kevin and me and said that to not follow *the pattern* was rebellion. She finished her sermon and it was now time for directive prophesy over the graduates.

What she said was completely opposite from what her husband, the apostle, had said years before and the graduates were very confused. In short, she was taking away my daughter and son-in-law and putting them in another church. She was placing our son-in-law's brother under Kevin to be mentored, then to take over pastoring our church.

After the service, she blatantly asked my husband, "Are you pleased with what the 'Lord' said?"

Kevin didn't hold back. "No, I'm really not", he said. "I don't understand why you would speak something different that would change everything that these graduates have prayed and worked for all these years."

That was the final nail in the coffin.

I Corinthians 14: 29 – 33 NKJV

[29]Let two or three prophets speak, and let the others judge. [30]But if anything is revealed to another who sits by, let the first keep silent. [31]For you can all prophesy one by one, that all may learn, and all may be encouraged. [32]And the spirits of the prophets are subject to the prophets.
[33]For God is not the author of confusion but of peace, as in all the churches of the saints.

She didn't go out to lunch with us to celebrate that afternoon. Instead, she took the woman who had been feeding her information, and one other woman to lunch. She obviously didn't care that we knew what was going on at this point. I was still thinking that this was a transient ordeal. We would work through it and everything would go back to normal.

Kevin was more concerned about the two young couples who were prophesied over than his own future. They had been shaping their lives toward a goal that was now as good as silly putty. We all believed when the apostle prophesied over them years before, it was of the Lord. Now what? Does the Lord change His mind over something like this?

After a few days, he did the unthinkable. He called the apostle on the phone. His wife answered the first time and told Kevin that the apostle wasn't available. Kevin left a message for him to please return the call.

When we hadn't heard anything after a couple of days, Kevin called a second time and she answered again. This time she and Kevin set up a meeting for the following Saturday.

Kevin got busy looking for the prophesies that the apostle had spoken and were written down. Everything had been recorded on paper and the words were nothing like his wife had spoken.

When Kevin called that Saturday, the apostle answered the phone. A couple had moved with the apostle and his wife when they retired, to be a help to them. The man was listening on the other line. The apostle's wife was sitting there by him, listening. Kevin read the prophesies that the apostle had spoken and then asked, "Why is this so contrary to what (your wife) said?"

Anything that was waiting for Kevin as far as ministry was concerned OR was presently being practiced, flew out the door at that moment. He had questioned the highest authority and was going to pay the price for it.

The conversation went on for several minutes and the end conclusion from the apostle was this, "We will just have to put all of this on God's clothes line and see what happens." One thing was for sure is. Whatever the end result turned out to be, would be Kevin's fault.

In the meantime, we continued to go through the motions of being in our place as pastor and pastor's wife. After about twenty-five years of living under the lawful fist of the apostle and running a church "just as", something had changed, something marvelous... Jesus had showed up.

He had been there the whole time, of course. We were just too deceived to see Him as He really is. Yes, the apostle talked about Jesus. Yes, the people in the church talked about Jesus. Here's the dilemma –Jesus - became a symbol not a person. You can't have a relationship with a symbol. The relationship was with the apostle.

My daddy knew that. He saw the charade. That's why he couldn't stay. Other people came for short periods of time and soon left. They saw it. Our myopic vision started to expand, and we began to see it too.

Kevin introduced videos to our congregation on Sunday night by Kirk Cameron about evangelism and talking to people about the Lord. We were expanding our vision to evangelize. We had Bible studies and were beginning to understand grace and mercy again. Being seven hundred miles away helped us to be different from what we had been taught.

This was totally contrary to the main church. In spite of the spies in our congregation that were relaying everything that was going on to the main church up north, we continued.

We became officially the epitome of rebellion.

The sweet calm waters of talking about the Lord to people without having to tell them they had to *do* all the other liturgy "in order to" be saved, born again or converted was dried up. This simple Gospel wasn't enough to be part of the remnant!

The blood of Jesus wasn't enough for this authority that we served under. The cross wasn't enough to kneel down in front of and be forgiven and then rise to a new way of life.

We should have realized that they would go as far as they did. Our minds never conceived the evil that was about to take place. We believed we were exempt. They wouldn't do to us what they had done to countless others. This wouldn't happen to *us*. We were wrong. We were *far past* the *beginning of the end.*

When someone did something that called for church discipline, the apostle always blamed the person committing the discretion. When someone left the "church" (either by their own volition or by expulsion) the apostle would always find a scapegoat whom he could blame. It was never about the spiritual abuse he wielded that caused them to leave. He always had a specific label that he gave to this person or persons to show *they* had sinned. He wanted to prove that *they* were out of the will of the Lord.

David Hayward has made a list of examples that show how the apostle would "turn the tables" so the church member was always at fault. The following is considered to be how the church member is accused of committing a sin.

1. questioning a leader's actions is interpreted as rebellious

2. doing other than exactly what you're told is interpreted as disobedience

3. questioning authority is interpreted as not submitting to authority

4. stronger offense creates stronger defense that is interpreted as obstinacy

5. talking about your questions with others is interpreted as divisive and seditious

6. knowing a leader is human with weaknesses is interpreted as disrespectful

7. when you decide the church is not healthy and leave is interpreted as unfaithful

8. thinking for yourself is considered maverick

9. trying to learn how to live your own life is considered immature and unruly

NAKEDPASTOR DAVID HAYWARD [11]

We were labeled every one of the "sins" listed above. We challenged the apostle's wife when she came to the graduation and she used her gift of deception to turn our church and our children against us.

It's not only that we couldn't believe that something like this would happen to us. We just couldn't believe that someone would be that evil in the name of Christianity. She was a wolf in sheep's clothing.

[11] www.beliefnet.com/faiths/christianity/5-warning-signs-of-a-cult..

The next Pastor's Conference was up north the following winter. All the pastors and their wives, except the church in the other country were there. I was in complete denial. I was just glad to see all my "good" friends. I missed fellowshipping with them, especially two of the ladies.

We visited in the apostle's wife's hotel room one morning, while the men got together. She was very cordial. I was admonished although I can't remember what for. I had learned to take her criticisms with a "grain of salt". They were just part of being in her presence. I must have dismissed it by the time I left her room. This was a drastic change from the previous twenty-three years. Normally, I would be a puddle on the floor.

The ladies planned to go to lunch together while the pastors met with the senior apostle and his wife. I thought we had a lovely time. Nothing seemed strange. There was no tension between anyone. We all rode in a large van together to get to the restaurant.

On the way back, we stopped by the apostle's son's house to drop off his wife. I got out of the van as well to give her a hug goodbye. She hugged me for the longest time. She looked at me, then said that she hoped she would see me again. Brushing off the comment, I said of course she would and gave her a big smile.

When we got back to the hotel Kevin met me at the door of the van and said, "We're leaving. Get your things." I was stunned. What had happened to cause this type of reaction in Kevin?

I remembered a phone conversation that I had had with my "sister" friend a few months prior. Both of our daughters were expecting their first babies and they were also good friends. I was so excited, and I was talking about how these little ones could grow up together and be friends as well. She said she *hoped* they would be able to. I said of course they would. I knew she was hinting about us leaving the church. But, I still thought that we were in control of that scenario. I believed we were "shun" proof. I was so naïve.

Initially, Kevin wouldn't tell me what happened. He said he couldn't talk about it right then. As we drove further down the road, away from the source of whatever was causing Kevin to be so disturbed, he opened up.

After the cordial beginnings, the apostle handed over the meeting of all the pastors, supposedly *his* pastors, to his wife and rolled out the door in his wheelchair. This was 2008. At the writing of this book, it was nine years ago. What she told me that day in the food court was developing but it wasn't from the Lord. I believe she had taken over by chiseling away at the apostle for years until only a shadow of what he had been remained. He was taking several narcotics (his words) and she was a nurse. She knew better but allowed it to continue.

She went around the room and told each pastor what they had done wrong and where they fell short. When she got to Kevin she told him that he hadn't been running the church in the right way for a long time. He didn't have a clue about what the Kingdom of God was about. She then said if he didn't start changing to pastor "that little church down there" according to the "pattern" (the way they wanted him to run the church) she would come "down there" and take *everything*.

She belittled each pastor for all to see. She deliberately humiliated each and every one of them in front of their peers...except for her son.

110

Testimonial of an Ex- Member from One of the Other Churches #4

Examples of Shunning /Family Separation we witnessed over the years.

* When somebody left, closed door congregational meetings were held. For example, at the end of services, visitors (if any) were dismissed, and sanctuary doors were closed. We were told from the pulpit not to contact the person. Not to associate with them.

* Phrases such as, "he's not one of us," "he left us," "he's deceived," "outside the camp," "not following the Truth," "turning his back on God's best," "you can't follow him" "keep yourself unstained from the world" were used regularly to justify the cutting of ties.

* From the pulpit, the pastor stated that he had cut his daughter, out of his will after she had left.

* "Some things are more important than family ties" was preached from the pulpit.

* It was preached from the pulpit regularly that your true family are the people in the church.

* People who had cut off family members, including children and parents, were held up as examples of right behavior, honored for their sacrifice.

* Parents cut off children who had left; children cut off parents; grandchildren were kept from their grandparents.

* The pastor and his wife came to be known as "dad" and "mom," "grandpa" and "grandma" by those who cut off their parents.

* Prayer meetings included prayers for the destruction of the well-being of people who left.

When people left "the church," their very existence was

blotted from memory. Pictures disappeared from homes. Young people were left out of yearbooks. Photographs were cropped so as not to include the wayward sons. Family members were left out of Christmas letters, their names not even listed among the remaining on the signature lines of cards, like they were not part of the family history. The names of the "prodigals" were not to be mentioned or discussed. Invitations were not extended to events such as weddings and birthday parties. "I have three children," proclaimed the pastor, who actually has four. Were these former members thought of as dead? No. When a loved one dies; the survivors strive to keep the memories of the deceased alive. Pictures remain, stories are told, memorials are created. In this destructive system, when someone chooses to leave, it is like they never existed.

Our family experience of shunning and the expectation to cut off our son while still members

* The expectation/pressure to cut off my son built up over time; it was not immediate.

* After he had stopped attending church, my son joined us for church on Mother's Day to honor me. Later that week, I was brought into the pastor's office and told that I should have called and asked if he could come. That my son's presence made people "uncomfortable." That if he wanted to come again, he would have to call the pastor first, and if he didn't, he would be escorted out.

* When we continued to reach out to and love our son, the pressure increased, from the members and the leadership.

* I was told that the correct "pattern" in dealing with a wayward son (defined as one who had left the church), was no contact.

* My daughter was told by a friend (11 years old) that my daughter was not allowed to speak my son's name in her presence.
* Planned get-togethers with my children's friends were cancelled because we associated with our son.
* I was told by a member that if we associate with my son, and if my children then talk about their time with my son to his children, his children will think there are no consequences for leaving the church. He didn't want his children to think they had "a choice."
* An elder told my husband that our house was a "place of darkness."
* One Tuesday night I sat at a picnic table during a church soccer get-together and not one person talked to me or approached me. No one. It was like I was invisible.
* Finally, I was brought into the pastor's office, without my husband or anyone else. That is when he told me it was time to "protect what I had left" - "Save my best" for God's people. He told me that he considers himself as having three kids (He has four. One has left the church). He told me that he does not understand why his daughter continues to send him cards on Father's Day. If she loved him, she would do what she was told (she was an adult), and follow the path that she was raised in. He told me that when she left, he told her that he "can't follow her." He told me that his remaining children think he did the right thing by cutting her off. He said that if I continue to include my son in family activities, such as holidays, birthday parties, etc. that I should expect that any members I invite would not attend. He said that if I continued to associate with my son, people would start to "dis-fellowship" me as well. I

started asking him about specific examples, such as "what if my son stops by on his way to or from class? Should I let him in? Give him a meal? Offer him a glass of water?" I was told no. Changing the locks was suggested. Submit a change of address card at the post office so I didn't have to contact him regarding mail received.

It was very, very frightening to leave, because we knew the consequences would be shunning. Everyone knows that. I felt I had three choices: 1) stay and cut off my son; 2) stay and refuse to cut off my son, but then have my young children ostracized and face the threat of "dis-fellowship." 3) Leave, and risk losing my oldest daughter. None of them were acceptable choices. All of them included damage to my family, my children. That realization is when I "snapped out of it," so to speak, and gained the courage to say, "I will no longer be part of a system that backs a mother into a corner and forces her to choose between her children. I will no longer raise my children like that. I will no longer be part of a system that so readily discards people. I will NOT turn my back on my son. I will stand for what is right, put it in God's hand, and let the chips fall where they may. We left in August 2012. Thankfully, my oldest daughter and her (now) husband, left 6 weeks later. God protected my family. We got out intact. We were one of the few "lucky ones."

When we told our children we were leaving, my then 12-year old son cried, "I don't want to leave God! I would rather live with (another family in the church) than leave God!" Even though we had never taught him to think along those lines, at his young age he had already internalized the mindset that that particular church = God, and that loyalty to that church and those members were more important than loyalty to his own, God-given family.

The Shunning we have experienced since we left

* It was immediate. No one, not one person, except my daughter, made any attempt to contact us, to talk to us, to hear our story, to ask why we're leaving.

* I wrote a letter to the church, explaining that we weren't leaving any of them as people, but rather we were leaving the system, and extending a hand of friendship to anyone remaining. I never got a response from anyone.

* I wrote letters to a couple of my very closest friends, explaining why we left, and extending a hand of friendship. I received one reply from my very best friend, the matron-of-honor at my wedding. It included only 4 lines. It ended with "for all involved, it would be beneficial to have a quick and complete break...Good bye." All other attempts to reach out were ignored.

* My children immediately lost all their lifelong friends. They couldn't understand what we had "done wrong" to make everyone hate us so much.

All relationships within the system, including family relationships, are conditional on the unconditional obedience and loyalty toward the leadership.

* The young woman who we had lined up to house and cat-sit for us while we were on vacation called and left a message on our answering machine just days before we were to leave and said she would not be able to watch our cats. She said she is sorry it has to be that way, but it does.

* On the day of my oldest daughter's move, my friend sat inside her truck in my driveway waiting for some things to be loaded. She made no attempt to reach out to me. When

I approached her to greet her, she turned her back on me. When I told her I loved her, she scoffed and refused to look at me.

* The only time anyone has attempted to contact me was when my (now) son-in-law decided to leave the church. His mother left a hostile, berating message on my answering machine accusing me of "destroying her family."

* My son-in-law's mother did not come to my daughter's bridal shower.

* My son-in-law's family (parents and brother) would not come to the wedding of their son and my daughter. They were invited, and we wrote them a letter begging them to come, but to no avail.

* When we saw a group of young teenagers at the Fourth of July fireworks, they literally turned up their noses and turned their faces from us when we passed on the sidewalk. This, apparently, is how they are taught to behave.

* A couple young people have contacted us since we left. At least one of them has been told by his parents that we are "dead to him" and he should "leave us that way." They told him that they would cut him off if he continued to associate with us.

When people left "the church," their very existence was blotted from memory. The names of the "prodigals" were not to be mentioned or discussed. Invitations were not extended to events such as weddings and birthday parties. "I have three children," proclaimed the pastor, who actually has four. Were these former members thought of as dead? No. When a loved one dies; the survivors strive to keep the memories of the deceased alive. Pictures remain, stories are told, memorials are created. In this destructive system, when someone chooses to leave, it is like they never existed.

Yes, it has always been like that. Was I aware of it? Yes. Was I a part of it? Yes. Did I ever question it? Challenge it? Yes, sometimes tearfully, sometimes with anger. What about forgiveness? Love? Reconciliation? Freedom to choose your path without fear of abandonment? I was told I didn't understand. I was rebellious. I was too independent. I was wrong. I was sinful because of my doubt. There was something wrong with my faith. It was the family's choice, I thought. So rather than rock the boat, and out of fear of "losing everything," I shut up and went along with it. Inside, I was heartbroken, angry, and slowly dying. Outside, I was an obedient sheep. But quietly, I made up my mind that if it was ever me, I wouldn't treat my loved ones like that. Although I went along with it for years, in my heart I never fully bought into it. My authentic- self rejected the pattern. I believe that is why I was able to leave. My "rebellious independence" set me free.

Not until it did happen to me did it rock my world enough to extricate myself. Not until it was in my face, and I was told that my family would be ostracized if I didn't cut ties with my own "prodigal son," was it enough for me to take a stand and say, "No!" I will no longer be a part of it. I was well aware of the consequences of that stand.

Here's the rub. All along, I trusted my friends. There were a few that I thought would always stand by me and my family, unconditionally. That is where I was wrong. All friendship, all relationships, including family relationships, are conditional in that system - conditional depending on the unconditional obedience to the leadership.

I take responsibility for my involvement and ask for forgiveness from all who have been hurt by my involvement, especially my own children. As I accept God's forgiveness, I strive to forgive myself. But now, I, for one, am thankful to no longer be counted among their numbers. And I, and my children, are now dead to them.

Chapter Eleven

The Beguiling Thread of Latter Rain
"You Become What You Behold"

I mentioned Latter Rain in the beginning of the book to help illustrate where the doctrines of this church I'm writing about came from. George Hawtin, who I referred to, was one of the early leaders but he had a predecessor.

I have told Kevin's and my story mostly, but before we continue, it's time for you to see the larger picture. There is a beginning to this deception, control and heresy that Kevin and I experienced.

The apostle did not begin the dysfunction in the church we were associated with. He perpetuated, condoned and supported it. The church where he was introduced to Latter Rain was not the beginning either, although it played a major role.

The church that the apostle came out of was Bethesda Missionary Temple where Myrtle Beall was pastor. **Myrtle D. Beall.** Sister **Myrtle** D. **Beall** was the 'spearhead' in bringing the Latter Rain Movement into the United States from Canada. The Lord gave her a word to "build an armory" in Detroit, Michigan and that she did! **Bethesda Missionary Temple** is known far and wide as a church of revival and visitation.[12]

Here is where we connect the dots. One of the major beliefs and doctrines in the churches we were associated with was "impartation". The apostle taught and emphasized that anything of any significance; ministry, water baptism, prophesy, spiritual gifts, etc., was imparted by the laying

---

[12] highlanderglory.net/myrtle-beall.html

on of hands by someone who had the authority and the experience to do so.

Whoever imparts is actually transferring what they have within their spirit to the person they are laying hands on. A Biblical example is when Moses laid hands on Joshua. (Joshua 1: 1-18)

Rev. William Branham, (1909 – 1965) a healing evangelist from the 1940's through 1960's, was credited by some, for starting the "Latter Rain" and "Word of Faith" movements as well as other fringe groups. In his teachings on Joel 2:23:

23Be glad then, ye children of Zion, and rejoice in the LORD your God: for he hath given you the former rain moderately, and he will cause to come down for you the rain, the former rain, and the latter rain in the first month.

He said the "latter rain" was the Pentecostal Movement of his day.

Spiritually speaking the beginnings of Latter Rain were set on feet of clay. Branham was a self - proclaimed prophet and also proclaimed himself the angel of Revelation 3:14 and 10:7.

Revelation 3:14 [14]And unto the angel of the church of the Laodiceans write; These things saith the Amen, the faithful and true witness, the beginning of the creation of God;
Revelation 10:7 [7]But in the days of the voice of the seventh angel, when he shall begin to sound, the mystery of God

should be finished, as he hath declared to his servants the prophets.

Branham taught that the Word of God was given in three forms: the zodiac, the Egyptian pyramids, and the written scripture. He said that anyone belonging to any denomination had taken "the mark of the beast".
He denied the Trinity, calling the Trinitatian doctrine "of the devil."
Branham > "Now don't get excited. Let me say this with Godly love. The hours approached where I can't hold still on these things no more... Trinitarianism is of the devil. I tell you that – Thus saith the Lord."
He insisted that believers baptized by a Trinitarian formula should be baptized in the name of "Jesus only."
William Branham, Footprints on the Sands of Time: The autobiography of William Marrion Branham, Part Two (Jeffersonville, IN: Spoken Word Publications, 1975), 606-7.
His doctrine of the "serpent's seed" taught that Eve's sin involved sexual relations with the serpent. Some humans are descended from the serpent's seed and are destined for hell, which is not eternal, however. The seed of God, i.e., those who receive Branham's teaching, are predestined to become the Bride of Christ. There are still others who possess free will and who may be saved out of the denominational churches, but they must suffer through the Great Tribulation.
Burgess and McGee, editors, *Dictionary of Pentecostal and Charismatic Movements* Zondervan Publishing House, Grand Rapids, Michigan. p.

When Branham was a small child he first heard the Voice. The Voice accompanied Branham throughout his lifetime, and eventually made itself known as an angel. This angel directed him in every aspect of his personal life, and **it was the angel rather than the Holy Spirit to whom Branham gave credit for his power.** (Kurt Koch, Occult Bondage and Deliverance, Grand Rapids: Kregel, 1972, p. 50).

Branham knew that if he didn't do what the Voice told him to do, he would suffer greatly. We believe Branham was influenced by demonic spirits. The bondage in which he lived was an occultic bondage. His powers were those of a soothsayer. His healing powers were occultic. The voices that tormented him, the vibrations and swellings in his hand, the lights, the fiery balls that supposedly danced about the room during some of his healing crusades, the complete exhaustion he experienced after his meetings--all of this is evidence of occultic powers. And this is what men of God tried to warn him of. In fact, when Branham met fortunetellers, they even told him that he was influenced by their kind of supernatural powers:

"What made me more scared than ever, every time I met a fortuneteller, they would recognize something had happened. And that would just ... it just nearly killed me. "For instance, one day my cousins and I was going down through a carnival ground, and we was just boys, walking along. So there was a little old fortuneteller sitting out there in one of those tents. ... She said, 'Say, you, come here a minute!' And the three of us boys turned around. And she said, 'You with the striped sweater' (that was me). ... "And

I walked up, I said, 'Yes, ma'am, what could I do for you?' "And she said, 'Say, did you know there's a Light that follows you? You were born under a certain sign. (Zodiac)' "I said, 'What do you mean?' "She said, 'Well, you were born under a certain sign. There's a Light that follows you. You were born for a Divine call'" (William Branham: The Man and His Message, pp. 22-23). Branham tells of other instances in which soothsayers told him similar things. He said, "And every time I get around one of them, that's the way it would be." Then the preachers, saying, "That's the Devil! That's the Devil!" (Ibid. p. 25).

Now we know that the Zodiac and the Pyramids (that Branham mentioned) play a huge part in the occult. So how on earth can the occult be equal to Scripture? Witchcraft, Astrology and New Age all use the pyramids and the zodiac for divination i.e., predicting the future. The pyramids are an essential holiday spot for occultists, witches, magicians, necromancers and many a demon/ spirit. The narrow passages through-out the pyramids allowed for occult soul travel were mummified Kings and other notable people were buried with gold, food and other worldly possessions in the belief that their soul would need these things in the after-life. Pyramids also have an occult alignment with the stars i.e., the Zodiac.

Let's see what the bible says about this: **Deuteronomy 18 v 9-12**

"⁹ When thou art come into the land which the LORD thy God giveth thee, thou shalt not learn to do after the abominations of those nations. ¹⁰ There shall not be found among you any one that maketh his son or his daughter to pass through the fire, or that useth divination, or an observer of times, or an enchanter, or a witch. [11] Or a charmer, or a consulter with familiar spirits, or a wizard, or a necromancer. [12] For all that do these things are an abomination unto the LORD: and because of these abominations the LORD thy God doth drive them out from before thee."

After Branham's death a tombstone in the shape of a pyramid was placed on his grave. On top of the tombstone is what appears to be an eagle, but it is in fact a Pheonix.

Definition of a phoenix- in classical mythology) a unique bird that lived for five or six centuries in the Arabian desert, after this time burning itself on a funeral pyre and rising from the ashes with renewed youth to live through another cycle.

[13] This is a sad story. It is too bad that Branham did not listen to the wise voices which were warning him that the visitations were demonic. It is too bad that Branham did not listen to his own fears and his own conscience which caused him to want to escape the visitations. It is too bad that Branham did not listen to the Bible. As it turns out, he did not listen to wisdom. Instead he allowed the demonic powers to control his life, and he, in turn, led multitudes of other people into all sorts of error and confusion. *https://www.wayoflife.org/free_ebooks/downloads/ William_Branhams_Bogus_Healings.pdf*

In 1955, Branham's career suddenly began to falter.[28] [29] Jim Jones, the founder and the leader of the Peoples Temple, best known for the mass suicide in November 1978, used Branham to springboard his own ministry. He organized a mammoth religious convention that took place

[13] https://www.discerningtheworld.com/2009/05/09/william-branham-false-prophet-2/

June 11 through June 15, 1956, at Cadle Tabernacle in Indianapolis. To draw the crowds, Jones needed a religious headliner, and so he arranged to share the pulpit with Branham.[30][31]

When Jim Jones needed a headline act for the opening of Peoples Temple in Indianapolis, Indiana, who better would fill the bill than William Branham.

In March 1956, when Branham announced a new campaign to be held for four days in June that year, Jones promoted the event through the *Herald of Faith* newsletter, the Open Door newsletter, local newspapers and mailing lists. The strategy was successful: Branham's name attracted some eleven thousand people to the Cadle Tabernacle, and the evangelist performed numerous miracles through his alleged gift of discernment which facilitated healing the sick. In the months to follow, Jones too, became a familiar name within the Healing Revival Movement for possessing the same supernatural gifts.

http://jonestown.sdsu.edu/?page_id=61481

Jones also visited Bethesda Missionary Temple in Detroit, Michigan. This is the same church the apostle, from the church we attended, came out of.

http://jonestown.sdsu.edu/?page_id=13157

We (Jones and his wife) decided that we would go to a convention in Detroit...to the Bethesda Temple. And I remembered at the time that I didn't want to go too much. And we were on the way, driving, and I'm one who never had very many supernatural things happen to me — and I never had any until I met and knew the ministry of JJ. But while I was thinking and even expressing my displeasure with making this strip to the Bethesda Temple and to the church convention, the words spoke in my mind, "You'll not be sorry my dear that you came here." And in fact, I wasn't sorry because it was an incident at Bethesda Temple in Detroit Michigan that really gave the opportunity to J to take his ministry further and reach more people with it. [14]http://jonestown.sdsu.edu/?page_id=13157

Branham and Jones believed they were Malachi 4 Elijah Prophets:

Malachi 4
5Behold, I will send you Elijah the prophet before the coming of the great and dreadful day of the LORD: 6And he shall turn the heart of the fathers to the children, and the heart of the children to their fathers, lest I come and smite the earth with a curse.

When Reverend William Branham prophesied of God's blessing of Reverend Jim Jones ministry during a joint Latter Rain healing campaign in Indianapolis, Indiana, he had no idea what he had started. As Jones took his place in line as a "Malachi 4 Elijah Prophet," a deadly chain reaction ended in the deaths of over 900 people during what would become known as the Jonestown Massacre.

All the above commentary is to help demonstrate to you, the reader, the dangerous thread that runs through the dysfunctional religious group, the cult, this book is about.

Here is my point:

[14] http://seekyethetruth.com/resources-deep-jones.aspx

* William Branham laid hands on Jim Jones and George Hawtin.
* George Hawtin laid hands on Myrtle Beall in Canada.
* Myrtle Beall Ministered with Jim Jones and she laid hands on the apostle of the church we came out of.

Everything from William Branham was imparted, passed down through the years where today it resides in the man that is called an apostle, in the Latter Rain church that we were a part of. It also resides in his wife and anyone that has accepted the call of ministry in their life from this couple.

Kevin and I pray for the people in leadership of this church every day to repent. We pray for them to ask forgiveness from the people whose lives have been torn apart, so lives can begin to be healed.

Kevin and I have asked forgiveness from the people whose life we effected by teaching the cultish doctrine. We have repented, prayed and continue to pray to renounce this doctrine and its heresy in our own lives. We are praying and begging God to do the same for our children.

Chapter Twelve

Comparative Cult Behavior

I have been learning about the church of Scientology to compare the differences and similarities between what they believe and practice with what this Latter Rain Church believes and practices.
Even though the origins are different, the under current that forms their philosophies is the same.

Scientology:
- Anything "bad" that happens is your fault. The leaders don't take responsibility for anything.

- You have to do research to find out questions you may have because you are not allowed to ask questions.

- Made to Disconnect from friends and family (shunning)

- Church is first, family is always second

- Mental abuse – rationalizing insanities i.e., being a Christian, you will be sent to outer darkness for being disobedient/Scientology – being labeled a suppressive person

- A fate worse than death when you leave/kicked out of the church

- The church will talk with and tell family and friends to shun you

- You are told by disconnecting, you are helping that person to come back to the church.

- When parent/child relationships are taken away, the church fills the role of the parent.
- If you voice concerns to someone they will turn you in.
- Members believe the church over their family members.
- When you voice your own thoughts and opinions, you are labeled reprobates doomed for outer darkness/or a suppressive person
- People go without to support the church and the leadership.
- They look for anything that they can twist to use against you.
- "You" desert your family when you leave the church. The church is never wrong, you are.
- Divorce is called for and considered the answer when either the man or the wife leaves the church.

If any of these points or any of the examples on this list of Scientology ring true with you, get out of wherever you're going to church as fast as you can. You will become a victim if you don't and you don't deserve to be punished. Get out, the sooner the better. This may ensure you will leave with your family intact.
[15]http://www.aetv.com/shows/leah-remini-scientology-and-the-aftermath
The paradigm of cultish behavior is the same. It doesn't matter that the above list comes from Scientology.

You could use the same list for any cult out there, past or present.

How do intelligent, financially secure, educated, professional adults fall into the snares of a cult? As I said in the beginning of this book, we were looking for something new, something exciting. We wanted to "belong" somewhere.

Once you think you've found the panacea to what you've been looking for, you're hooked. As the requirements are gradually fed to you, they are in sequential to what you are experiencing initially. By the time the "control factor" takes over, the end justifies the means. You've adopted the belief system and it has become a part of who you are.

When Kevin and I thought about leaving, we believed we would "miss God". We thought we were led to the church for a reason and we didn't want to be disobedient. We had received "the truth" from a man that was an "apostle". We were now part of the remnant and were the sons of God. Yet, over time, there was something deep inside that was causing us to doubt, continue to question. He was... the Holy Spirit.

Another couple that we were close to were having the same doubts. We supported each other's concerns and questions. We prayed together, begging for discernment. We were on the same page. How could we put a man before God?

They were stronger than we were. They got out. It was painful, but they counted the costs and left. Today, they are spiritually strong, and their family is intact. Comparatively, we suffer from PTSD and our children have shunned us.

We **did** leave once, after our friends left. We even visited other churches. There was always something missing. The co-dependency that we had learned to rely on was absent. The pleasing and being rewarded for obedience weren't there in these other churches. We had been conditioned. We had been brain washed to look toward spiritual "control". To be able to think and decide for ourselves was gone. It had been erased.

We thought we could find God elsewhere. But it wasn't God we were looking for. He was surely there in these other churches.

It was the praise for our sacrifice that we were looking for. The sacrifice of ourselves, our dreams and our desires that we had given up was worn as a spiritual medal.

We were upside down in this abstract definition of the Kingdom of God. Knowing now what I didn't know then, "our" sacrifice was truly irrelevant. The sacrifice of our Lord, Jesus Christ, is what mattered. It's all that mattered. We had been blinded to God's truth. We were myopic by viewing and practicing man's narcissistic doctrines. We hungered and thirsted for validation by reading the apostle's written material instead of the unadulterated truth of the living Word of God.

Sadly, the above was not realized until much later. We agreed to a final meeting with the apostle when there was a fund raiser at the church. It was late Summer, and we found ourselves going back to what had become familiar. We knew that we would be called on the carpet and intimidation tactics would be used. We were willing to put ourselves through the mental and spiritual abuse that was inevitable.

My stomach was in knots as we drove down the road

that lead to the church. As we approached the parking lot, I thought I was going to be sick. We walked into the fellowship hall and sat down. Thankfully, there weren't many people there. This was not the time to be greeted back by the congregation when we had not yet spoken with the apostle.

A couple did come over to say hello and sat down at the table with us. I looked around and there was the apostle's wife walking toward me. She asked me to come sit with her. She had something to talk with me about. Kevin wasn't invited.

No niceties were exchanged. She went straight for my Achilles heel, my oldest daughter.

"You know" she said, "That your daughter won't be able to return to the (church) school this fall if you remain where you are. You have to make a decision today."

She had me. She knew exactly where to strike, and she didn't hold back. There was no way that I would send our daughter back to the public schools. She had already experienced one when we first moved there. She was bullied. I knew I had to get her out of the public system. The school, that was a part of the church, seemed to be the perfect place for her now. She had been attending there for a couple of years, had made friends and was doing very well academically. I didn't have time to think about Christian schools as an alternative. My head was spinning. We had to make a decision right then.

Within five minutes Kevin and I were ushered into the apostle's office. There were some elders there, as well. One elder, in particular, was very harsh and we got the feeling that he would have thought it was just fine if we decided to stay out of the church. Who did we think we were to ever question his apostle?

We were contrite and asked for forgiveness. We asked to be forgiven! How convoluted is that? But we knew by then how to play the game. The members were always wrong, never the apostle or his elders. Here we were, right back in again.

Looking back at that time with contempt, I was relieved. Kevin was too. We were just amazed that they took us back. It felt right. We felt special. We were being accepted. That was truly the exception in this church. Spiritual and emotional abuse had become our normal.

Short sightedness is a virtue when you are a part of a cult. You are taught that you only need to see as far as the apostle allows you to see. Perspective is a luxury that you deny yourself just to be able to keep your head above water each day, each minute, each second at a time.

"A part of", "belong to" – these are verbs that describe the false sense of security that you are offered. They are oxymorons that are exposed when the curtain is drawn back and the real motive and personality of the apostle is uncovered. Narcissistic power yielding to unadulterated allegiance from the congregation is the equation.

Insight into character comes from listening intently to the spoken word. The physical person, their charisma, charm and dramatic flair is more often used to persuade audiences, as they use these stealth tools of disguise and deception.
Maximillian Degenerez

http://www.brainyquote.com/quotes/quotes/m/
maximillia636151.html?src=t_deception [16]

We weren't listening "intently" to what was being said by the apostle. We just wanted to be accepted by this charismatic, delusive leader.

If we had only known about the list in the beginning of this chapter then, it would have saved us the heartache and inapprehensible tragedy of a destroyed family.

---

[16] http://www.brainyquote.com/quotes/quotes/m/maximillia636151.html?src=t_deception

135

Testimonial of an Ex-Member # 5

My family is Jewish. My mother's family was Orthodox, but we were Conservative, which means we didn't follow the strict dietary rules and were much less formal. From a very young age I began questioning my faith and that led me to go to Israel in 1970 to live and work on a kibbutz. I was 19. Even there my questions persisted. "Does God hear me? Does He care what I think or do? If I pray in Hebrew and don't know what I'm saying, does it count?"

When I came back to the U.S. I worked with a girl who was what we called back then a Jesus Freak. She would tell me about Jesus and when I told her I was Jewish she told me about Old Testament prophecies of the Messiah. That led to my accepting Jesus and joining a church of mostly young people called the Pittsburgh Christian Fellowship. Over the years the name would change several times.Today it is called *************. It was a non-denominational New Testament Church.

The pastor was a charismatic leader and we were all excited to follow his lead, but over the years he became more of a ruler and less a leader. The church leadership controlled more and more of our lives to the point where we no longer had friends outside the church. Even family relationships with non-church members was discouraged. If a family member left the church, we were not to fellowship with them unless they repented and were "restored"....and we went along with it for 35 years.

My husband and I volunteered in the church school. He taught Drama. I aided in various classrooms for 25 years. Our children attended the school from day 1 and both graduated there. Parents could be teachers and aides, but we had no say in how the school was run. We were to be obedient sheep as in all other activities. Sometimes the church authority would actually undermine relationships between parents and their children. My husband took me to a concert at the Civic Arena and when the pastor heard about it, he criticized our "bad judgement" to our daughter in front of her friends in the cafeteria rather than come and tell us.

Another instance in my life. The pastor's wife would call me at work and criticize my husband. One day she told me that our daughter, who was serving at another church plant at the time, was furious with her dad. This was news to me. I asked what she was angry about and the pastor's wife said that she was not at liberty to discuss it! That led to my daughter and husband being estranged for quite a while. When we were all finally out of Lakeview I asked her why she had been so angry. She said that she never was! The pastor's wife told her that her dad was the one who was angry.

Families were destroyed by that woman and none of us stood up to her because we all had pledged submission to church leadership.

For us it came to a head, finally, when the pastor's wife called and was so totally out of line that my husband hung up on her. That led to our being told not to come back to church. We were shunned. No one asked us why. Total submission- if leadership said we were gone- it was as if we had never lived.

I still have nightmares from time to time. Most concern the pastor's wife, but not as often these days. We are out 12 years now.

Chapter Thirteen

The Meeting

Kevin had now pastored a church in a southern city for eighteen years. The church that we were trained in up north and had an "association" with, sent three pastors to town, two from the main church and one from another church we were in association with.

They came to us for the sole reason of declaring that my husband was no longer fit to pastor. How they came to this life altering conclusion would be short of reason to the mainstream Christian. But the reasons that these men had, made perfect sense in their alternate universe of pseudo spirituality.

First, we had been teaching the Evangelism Class and showing videos of Kirk Cameron. These videos showed examples of how to witness. We were being taught by someone outside the church.

Second, we were aiming for North Carolina. The prophesies Kevin had received over the years pointed to him establishing churches in the South. We believed the Lord had led us to North Carolina through treatment for my Lyme Disease.

The apostle had been on the same page in the beginning. He was fine with us holding a Bible study and "testing the waters". His wife was not, however, and Kevin was very soon labeled as a rogue pastor, hungry for the apostolic place of authority.

We believed the Lord was speaking to us directly about this calling and we were willing to go against authority to make sure it happened. So, I suppose the apostle's wife was correct.

Looking back, it's a blessing that we didn't start a church in North Carolina. We would have been preaching and teaching flawed doctrine, heresy.

Third and the most detrimental - Kevin didn't agree with the apostle's wife when she prophesied over those two young men in our church in opposition to what the apostle had said.

Whether any of that prophesy was true, including the original prophesy that these men had received from the apostle himself, is moot at this point. Would God speak through a "prophet" that was believing and teaching heresy? Even our own prophesies that provided a goal for us and we were aiming for with break neck speed was in question.

I had been in Kansas City for three months undergoing treatment for Lyme disease. I remember sitting in the treatment chair at the clinic. A concoction of medication was flowing into my veins. Kevin called me and told me that three pastors were coming down and he believed were going to try and take the church.

They had been there for two days by the time I received permission from the doctor and was able to fly home. Meetings between these three men and my husband had taken place that I was not yet privy to. They deliberately came down when I was still in Kansas City. It was a known fact that Kevin and I were stronger when we were together.

I got on a plane believing that we would stand our ground. Kevin and I had talked about leaving the church in August. This meeting I was heading for was in May. I truly believed that our church could cut the ties from the apostle and remain intact. We couldn't continue to enable the abusive nature of the leadership. We "wouldn't" put the apostle before the Lord anymore.

Over the years, Kevin has told me bits and pieces about those two days and nights when he was raked over the coals. I didn't know the full story until I began writing this book. He kept everything imprisoned in his heart. That's what people who have been abused do. They think it's their fault.

Through my Lyme treatment we developed an affinity toward North Carolina and the people. The apostle knew all about it. Kevin had every intention of continuing to talk with him about our plan, step by step.

At the time, we really believed that this plan was from the Lord. We were going through with it whether the apostle agreed or not. We made a decision to leave the association. August was our target date to get out and away from what we had been practicing for twenty-three years.

I believe that the Lord was trying to teach us to hear from Him again instead of man. Gradually we were deviating from the cultish doctrines and were moving more toward what the Bible had to say on how to walk out our Christianity. The scales were falling away, and our vision was becoming clearer.

Of course, the members of our church would be invited to stay with us. If they decided not to leave the cult, there would be a home for them in the other churches. All we knew is that we could no longer stifle the commandment of the "Great Commission". Jesus said to tell others about Him. That's what we intended to do.

Before these men came down, Kevin continued to sense that something was stirring up North. The last Pastor's Conference had been a nightmare. The apostle's wife had threatened us in the past. She said if you don't start doing what you're told, everything will be taken from you.

Considering the climate of our situation, Kevin wrote an addendum to one of the bylaws a week before the arrival of the pastors. He called a board meeting with our elder and our eldest son-in-law to vote on adding the addendum. He wanted to address the part where it stated that the leadership could come and take everything. He wanted to add that there should be a period of time when the pastor and the leadership (apostle) could sit down and talk things out.

Both men refused to vote in favor of the addendum. Kevin didn't push it. He thought that either they were intimidated or scared to change anything the apostle had sanctioned – or – they knew something he didn't. We trusted both of these men implicitly. It had to be the former.

That night after the men arrived, they and Kevin met in the conference room at the church. Kevin told them very candidly what he thought the Lord was speaking to him regarding ministry. They then attacked him with their words. The conversation went something like this:

"You have no idea what the Kingdom of God is! You don't preach well or manage the church well! Your people are starving!" The associate pastor, who was our younger son-in-law's father, was seething with contempt.

"We want you to take some time off. We'll use the excuse that your wife has been sick." The apostle's son (who was now the pastor/apostle of the main church) offered.

"What is going to happen to the church?" Kevin asked. (meaning the people)

"We don't have anyone to send."

This was a bad omen. They meant they were either going to close the building until they could send someone or try to sell it and take the people. As the discussion continued we feared for the worse.

The apostle's son continued.

"You will go on a probation period for right now."

"How long?"

"We don't know."

"Am I going to be able to minister again?"

"That depends on you."

At that juncture of the conversation the reason for this meeting was beginning to become very evident. Kevin was being told to acquiesce by forfeiting everything; the church, his ministry but most of all his rediscovered Lordship with Jesus. That meant, if he agreed to their proposal, he would stay in the association churches, sit in a pew, and be obedient to the apostle for the rest of his life.

He had been a pastor for twenty years. The thought of giving up what he considered to be the Lord's will at the time was too much.

"I'm done."

"What do you mean by that?" the apostle's son asked.

"I'm done. I'm finished.

The apostle's son said," You know we can take your keys."

"I know."

At this point, there was some discussion about the

financial management of the building, loan and bank accounts.

"Who is the guarantor? Who signed the loan?" the associate pastor asked.

"I did", Kevin said.

The associate pastor's – jaw dropped.

"It's in your name?" he asked in disbelief.

"I didn't want the people to be burdened. They have done enough already. I trusted the Lord to take care of everything."

Kevin didn't want to tax the people. They had spent five years of their lives building our church and he didn't want to put them through anything else. He was looking after his flock, a trait that was said by these three pastors that he didn't have.

Kevin got up to walk out. The pastor from the other church said,"We're not going to have any trouble with you are we?"

"You won't have any trouble out of me," Kevin said as he was walking through the door.

"We'll come to your house and get the check book and the articles of incorporation", the apostle's son called out as he got up out of his chair to follow Kevin.

When Kevin entered the hallway, the apostle's son was right behind him.

"That was the wrong reaction."

Kevin was spent. The reprimand was too familiar. For the last twenty-three years he had dealt with intimidation, manipulation and dysfunction. They had taken a toll on him. The ultimate control of this cult raised its ugly head.

He reverted to the only thing he had practiced throughout those twenty-three years - resignation.

Kevin fell to his knees and pleaded, "What do you want me to do? I submit to you. I'll do anything to make things right."

The apostle's son was not moved.

"You go home and wrestle with the angel tonight and we'll call you with a decision in the morning."

Wrestle with the angel. As if this dilemma was up to Kevin. But wrestle with the angel he did. And – he is still walking with a limp.

The three men followed Kevin home and collected the church checkbook, documents, all the keys and the articles of incorporation. At some point during all the activity of stripping Kevin of his dignity, we believe our elder, who had been with us for eighteen years, told the three men about Kevin wanting to change the bylaws. When the men heard this, it's not a surprise what was said on the phone when the apostle's son called Kevin the next morning.

"We heard about the bylaws. We've decided you can't come back. We'll meet at the church tonight and settle everything."

The fact that Kevin wanted to change the bylaws to make situations more amiable between churches was not even considered. The idea of changing them period was the offense. What Kevin had meant for good, was misconstrued and considered as an act of rebellion.

I flew in the next day. I really didn't find out all that happened in the meeting from the night before until I started writing this book.

When I arrived home, I hadn't seen my children in three

months. My oldest daughter came over to the house with my three grandchildren. I was exhausted but nothing and I mean nothing was going to interfere with the reunion of my babies. My youngest, my son was there at the house. He still lived with us. He was twenty. My middle daughter, the one who was expecting a baby, didn't come over but I didn't think much about it at the time. As I mentioned earlier, my son-in-law, her husband's father was one of the three men who had come down for the meeting. He was and is the assistant pastor of the main church. I assumed they had made plans and she would be over soon.

I soon found out that a corporate meeting had been called and we along with the whole church were to be there.

When we got to the church, we saw that there was a very one-sided assembly where the three pastors sat on the platform near the pulpit while we and the rest of leadership, including our family, sat in the chairs for the congregation. We were on the right side of the sanctuary and our elder and his family was on the left along with the rest of our children. The apostle's son stood and began to site allegations of why my husband was to be removed from ministry.

We were in survival mode – we didn't show emotion even if we disagreed with what was being said. We wouldn't give them the satisfaction. I wanted to say something. I wanted my husband to say something. Accusations from twisted, false pretenses had been formulated by these men and their superiors.

He was labeled a liar, incompetent, rebellious. His people were spiritually anemic. Everything that was said came down to the fact that he wasn't following the pattern. Kevin! Stand up! Tell him he's wrong! My mind was reeling. Eighteen years of ministry...gone. My husband had no fight left in him. In those two previous days they had emotionally and mentally beaten him until he was just a shell.

We were not given an opportunity for rebuttal. Kevin was ousted without any defense allowed on our part. When this man had finished with his accusations, he asked for anyone who wanted to resign from the church to write a short letter stating that decision.

The letters were written then and there and handed in to the pastors. Then the apostle's son, the one who was supposed to be an apostle himself, asked those who had written a resignation to stand and walk toward the back of the church.

I couldn't believe what I saw. My heart seemed to stop beating. I was *dizzy*. My mind was spinning with unbelief. There was my middle daughter and her husband, who had been like a son to us, moving along in line toward the door of the church. She was six months pregnant at the time with my grandson.

As I stood there and watched her walk away from me and her dad and through the church door, I ached with desperation. Should I run after her? I looked at Kevin. He had devastation written all over his face and he was looking down at the floor. Her husband had received his marching orders. He held my baby tightly to himself as they shuffled forward. I knew she wasn't *mine* anymore.

I hadn't seen or talked with her in three months due to me being away for treatment. Three months has turned into ten years.

Our elder and his family also stood. As they were walking down the aisle past us, I reached for his hand. He snatched it away and gave me a look of disgust. I was stunned and hurt. He had been like a brother to me. What had been said to them to make this OK? What had they said to themselves?

The pastor ended the meeting with something like this, "The Spirit of the Lord has departed from this place. It is now tainted."

I wanted to scream out "Liar!" But I couldn't say anything. My mouth was sealed shut.

I looked around for my other two children. Thank God they were still there. My youngest was bent over the pew, sobbing. His girlfriend, later to be wife, was trying to comfort him but she had an expression of desperation and shock on her face. My eldest and her husband, also like a son to me, were shaken, especially about their sister leaving.

"She'll be back", I managed, falling into a shelter of denial. "She'll come to her senses. She knows better."

She didn't. She's had four children since she left... four other precious grandchildren that I haven't seen, touched our even heard.

What do you do when you have to choose between a man that facilitated the loss of twenty-three years of your life? A man that says he IS as Jesus, knowing if you side with him you are turning your back on the one true Lord, Jesus Christ? If He, the true Jesus, is truly your Lord and Savior, there is no choice.

When we finally headed toward the exit, we entered the foyer and there on the table were the articles of corporation, the checkbook, the bylaws and the keys. There wasn't a note or any form of explanation. They obviously had confirmed earlier that day that Kevin was the soul guarantee on the loan.

This was a supernatural example of the Lord interfering, assisting or even changing the destiny of man. Kevin had no idea when he signed that loan that he was protecting the building. He just wanted to be a good steward.

At this point saving the building was nothing but a tangible reminder of what we had truly lost.

The fatalities were just beginning.

Chapter Fourteen

*"The time when there is nothing at all in your soul except
a cry for help may be just that time when God can't give it:
you are like the drowning man who can't be helped because
he clutches and grabs. Perhaps your own reiterated cries
deafen you to the voice you hoped to hear."*[17]

C.S. Lewis, *A Grief Observed*

The next day, after the meeting, Kevin and I had to fly
back to Kansas City to get my belongings and my car. Our
heads were spinning. Everything was happening so fast!
There was no time to thoroughly think about anything that
had happened.

We were clueless. We were believing that our middle
daughter would come to her senses. We believed that
our other two children would stand firm by our side. We
believed they would not waiver considering the three
pastor's accusations. There was no way our family would
fall apart.

We didn't take into account that our son had been in the
church his whole life, our middle daughter since she was
two and our oldest daughter since she was nine. They had
been totally indoctrinated. The fear, the power of deception
wielded by the leadership of that place, trumped our family
relationships.

Our children believed they were pleasing Jesus by
accepting what the pastors said, without question. This cult
had taken the pure love of our Lord and morphed it into
something dark. The leadership of these churches were
self-serving, revengeful, malicious, greedy imposters for

the true Kingdom of God and they called this darkness light.

The apostle taught that if any church didn't believe the doctrine that "they" held true, those churches would not inherit the Kingdom of God. Ultimately, that encompassed all the other churches in Christendom. The apostle and leadership called the people that attended these churches "nominal" Christians.

The first full day we were in Kansas City, my son-in-law, married to my eldest, called and said that they were leaving us. He said they were going back up north to one of the satellite churches. They had gotten "a word" from the Lord and believed this was the right thing to do.

In this cult, getting a word from the Lord meant flipping through the pages of the Bible and landing on a verse. When you stopped filtering through all the scriptures, there would be a verse that you believed applied as an answer to your situation. Today we call that "Bible roulette".

The very next day I received another call and was told by our son-in-law again, that my youngest, our son, was also leaving. He was twenty at the time, on the verge of his twenty-first birthday.

My son-in-law said that our son didn't want to be the one who made the call. He knew we would talk him out of it. We were close, you see. Kevin and I were close with all our children. We spent just about every weekend together, and nights during the week.

When I heard the words, two days in a row, that my other two children were gone, something snapped inside me. I screamed out in visceral pain for what seemed an eternity. I knew how the insidious manipulation, especially when it came to decision making, would control our children's thoughts. I remember wailing, in the passenger seat of our car. I wanted and tried, to crawl under the dashboard. I wanted to die. My cries were coming from the very core of my being. Everything I was, who I was, began to disappear with each gut-wrenching sob. Finally, after what seemed like days, I sat in that passenger seat of our car, silent and totally empty.

Kevin didn't know how to comfort me. He couldn't have if he had tried. He knew that. All he could do was sit there, in just as much pain, alone, helpless.

I left sanity that day and didn't return for months, even years to come.

Our three children and three grandchildren were our lives. Two days, surely, we could get back before anything else happened...we were wrong.

"I'll come down there to that little rebel church and take everything," still resounds in my mind, my soul, my spirit. These men were just instruments for her wrath. There was no room for any compassion in these men's hearts. They knew what they were doing and reveled in the twisted obedience of it.

These people held the keys to our lives and everyone's life that was inside that cult. Fear was the main reason that people were paralyzed. The doctrine of Outer Darkness was used repeatedly to keep them in line.

The chance that one would end up there because of not obeying the apostle was ingrained into their psyche. The words, "Depart from me. I never knew you." would be spoken by Jesus and the "believer" would dwell in outer darkness for eternity.

This is an example of how this "man" twisted scripture to keep people from leaving. Fortunately, Kevin and I never bought into that one. We were ready to leave but they got to us first. They wanted to make sure that we were put to shame, that our name was smeared, and our reputation altered beyond repair.

We were seven hundred miles away from the main church and we had started to "wake up" from the brain washing. We had begun to put back into our minds those things that had been "washed away". The main thing we regained was our realization that Jesus had saved us. It didn't matter how many times we were baptized in Jesus' name. We knew the cross is what mattered.

I was broken, body soul and spirit. But I was able to hold onto a splinter of the cross. I knew through the fog that Jesus was still there and that one day He would be in my life like He was when I first met Him.

I don't remember much from the first two to three years after it all happened. Kevin's sister and brother-in-law, Ted and Reenie Townley were critical in helping to save our lives. I do remember Reenie calling me every day for about a year, to make sure that I was alright. She still does.

When I say, "save our lives" I mean that literally. Once, when we were driving down to the beach through "no man's land" Kevin kept passing cars erratically. Normally, I would get onto him for doing that. But, not this time. We didn't care. Neither one of us cared if we died that night.

We would talk from time to time about driving into a brick wall. We wanted to go together.

The pain was so intense that we wanted to do "anything" to stop it. But God...He was still in control, even when we

154

weren't. His angels went before us despite our pain and often doubts of if God was even there. He was. He is. And I know now, He will be... throughout eternity.

Craig Branch was another beacon that offered hope through the darkness. He introduced Kevin into proper Bible study with apologetics which included exegesis and hermeneutics. With these tools, Kevin ultimately unraveled the false doctrine we were taught. Kevin was able to dispute all of it by God's word because of Craig.

I know Kevin was just as devastated as I was, but he kept putting one foot in front of the other. I don't know how he did it, but he did. He did it for me.

We had lost all three children within three days. In a fog, we left Kansas City and started driving in the direction of home but knew we couldn't go back. Not yet. It was if the car was on auto pilot. From this point I don't remember much. I just remember ending up in Cades' Cove outside of Gatlinburg, Tennessee, in the middle of a meadow...lost.

Chapter Fifteen

Shunned

But Peter and the apostles answered, "We must obey God rather than men." Acts 5:2 NKJV

When it came time for our grandchild to be born (my middle child's first baby), my good friend up north called me and told me my daughter was in labor. (There were "moles" in the churches who would let those who had left know important information.)

We hurried into the car and made a trip to the hospital. I had a relapse of Lyme or it could've been grief but due to the trauma of losing my children, I was in a wheel chair again. We didn't really think, we were just focused on getting to the hospital.

When we got there, the baby had been born. Kevin rolled me in and there was my little girl who had just given birth and I wasn't there. My son was holding the baby, it was a boy. I asked if I could hold him and my daughter looked at my son as to give him to me. Then, her husband said no. His dad was there and his mother. The same man who had been at the meeting and took our people and children from us.

He told us to leave. We didn't. Then he went to get security or a nurse, anyone who would throw us out of my daughter's and grandchild's room. As the nurse came in, you could tell she was upset with the man, I told Kevin to roll me out. I didn't want to upset my daughter more than she had already been.

I didn't get to hold her, hug her, touch her. The only consolation is that when I smiled at my son while he was holding the baby, he smiled back. His fiancé had to leave the room because of the tension that the man was causing. I saw her in the hallway as Kevin was rolling me by. I hugged her and told her that I loved her. She hugged me back.

She and my son are now married and have three children. They attend one of the churches.

When Kevin and I got to the car, I could feel that visceral pain again. It was so deep inside of me. I couldn't breathe, I couldn't talk, all I could do was scream in torment. Oh God!! How long? How long? Again, there was nothing that Kevin could do or say to comfort me. All he could do was clinch the steering wheel and keep the car on the road. He drove me home.

This wasn't the only time that I tried to see my daughter and wasn't allowed. She was more accessible than my other two. She lives where the main church is, and we have friends there.

Once, Kevin and I found out where she was living. This wasn't long after they moved up there from where we lived. She answered the door and screamed. My little girl screamed when she saw us. She spoke with us for a few minutes through the screen door, but wouldn't let us in. I could see my grandson sitting on a pallet on the floor.

She finally said she had to go and we left. When her husband got home, he was with that evil man, his dad and they called the police. We went to the police station and explained the whole story to them. They understood completely and wished us well.

I called my oldest daughter that night and her husband answered the phone. He was one of the young men who had graduated from the seminary school that I mentioned earlier, one of the men whom Kevin took up for. He was truly like a son to us. He was trying to be civil, then my oldest daughter took the phone and yelled into it, "Leave us alone!! You're not welcome here!! Don't come to *our* door!!"

I could hear my son-in-law trying to calm her down, but it was to no avail. She hung up the phone. I was at my best friend's house and I just had to leave – right then. My friend tried to help. She tried to make us stay but I was done. Twice in one day. Would the nightmare ever be over?

Then, once again, when my middle daughter had her second baby, we went up north and I bought gifts for the children. I just wanted to give them something from their Babby and Pappy.

I asked Kevin to just let me off at her house. I hoped she wouldn't call the police this time, but the chances were that she would. So, I didn't want to have a way to leave. I was ready to be arrested. I wanted her to see her mother be taken into custody for wanting to give her grandchildren gifts. I wanted her to see me in handcuffs.

When I knocked on the door, she wouldn't answer, but I could hear that she was there. I begged, "Please let me give these gifts to my grandbabies. Please *******! Please open the door!! I promise I want stay long!"

She stuck her hand outside the door signaling 5 minutes. I had 5 minutes to get out of there before the police came. I wasn't budging.

The police car drove up a few minutes later. I stood like

a statue on the porch. He came up to me and said, "Mam', please come with me."

"Are you going to arrest me?" I sobbed.

"No mam'. Just please come get in the car."

"Please arrest me." I begged.

"I'm not going to arrest you", he said. "You need to come with me. Where is your car?"

"My husband let me off."

"I'm going to take you to your husband."

I finally acceded. I went with him and got in the car. I don't remember much after that. I don't even remember getting to Kevin. I just hoped that my daughter was peeping through the window watching. I hoped that she was watching her mother, who loved her so deeply, be taken away by the sergeant of the police department.

I haven't mentioned our son. He was off the grid. My oldest and her husband were protecting him. He changed his cell phone number and I didn't know where he was living. I suspected with my oldest daughter, but I didn't know for sure. There was no way to get in touch with him.

I didn't hear his voice until about seven years later. I decided to call him at work. He was an RN at the time and I found out what hospital he was working in. He answered the phone saying his name.

"Hi Sweetheart".

Silence

"Please don't hang up."

"What do you want Mom?"

"I wanted to hear your voice. How are you?"

"I'm good."

"I just want you to know that we miss and love you and

160

that will never change."

"I have to go, I'm at work."

"I love you."

"I love you too."

It slipped out. He told me he loved me, and I've been holding on to those words ever since.

Once, I called him a while later before the holidays last year and asked if we could see him and our grandchild. He only had a little boy at the time. He said he didn't know. He would have to see.

When I called him again to get an answer he was angry and said he hadn't had a chance to talk to anybody about it. In other words, he needed to get permission.

I have called one last time when he wasn't in his office and left a message. I haven't heard a word.

Once I tried to open communication with my oldest daughter by writing a hand-written letter. There is significance in my reasoning. I wanted her to know that I was getting as close as I could get to her by hand writing instead of typing. She could touch the ink of my pen, remember and recognize my style of penmanship. She would realize the time and effort that I used for her. She has blocked my phone number and works at the school in one of the satellite churches.

One day when I was getting the mail, I saw her return address on an envelope. I was stunned. I just stood there and looked at it reading it over and over again to make sure it was true. I hurried inside and opened it. It was hand written and there was a Christmas photo of the whole family.

I carefully studied every face. I hadn't seen my

grandchildren in seven years. They had changed so much! My daughter and son-in-law looked the same. When it all sunk in, I laid my head down on the table and cried my heart out.

The letter was upbeat and talked about how there had been many times that they had struggled with meeting us somewhere, but each time the Lord said no. The Lord? The same Lord who sanctioned family before the church? Their pastor was saying no from the pulpit and they didn't want to go against his words.

I wrote her back and mentioned the apostle's wife's name once in regard that I was taught to do "just as" she did. She didn't write me back. I have recently sent her a card telling her how much I loved her.

I said, "I have loved you from the first time you sparked a light in my womb."

I changed my life for her and have never regretted it.

Now we are considered a dangerous threat to the church. Kevin and me along with our best friends that were kicked out, the ones that were so popular with the young people, have caused a policeman to sit in the foyer of their church during the meetings. The ushers are armed with tasers.

Has Kevin been that angry? Has he wanted to walk in and confront those two pastors that caused us so much pain? Yes. Would he? Never. What's the answer?

Luke 10: 25 – 37 – The Parable of the Good Samaritan NKJV
25 On one occasion an expert in the law stood up to test Jesus. "Teacher," he asked, "what must I do to inherit eternal life?"

²⁶ "What is written in the Law?" he replied. "How do you read it?"

²⁷ He answered, "'Love the Lord your God with all your heart and with all your soul and with all your strength and with all your mind'[a]; and, 'Love your neighbor as yourself.'[b]"

²⁸ "You have answered correctly," Jesus replied. "Do this and you will live."

²⁹But he wanted to justify himself, so he asked Jesus, "And who is my neighbor?"

³⁰In reply Jesus said: "A man was going down from Jerusalem to Jericho, when he was attacked by robbers. They stripped him of his clothes, beat him and went away, leaving him half dead. ³¹A priest happened to be going down the same road, and when he saw the man, he passed by on the other side. ³²So too, a Levite, when he came to the place and saw him, passed by on the other side. ³³But a Samaritan, as he traveled, came where the man was; and when he saw him, he took pity on him. ³⁴He went to him and bandaged his wounds, pouring on oil and wine. Then he put the man on his own donkey, brought him to an inn and took care of him. ³⁵The next day he took out two denarii[c] and gave them to the innkeeper. 'Look after him,' he said, 'and when I return, I will reimburse you for any extra expense you may have.'

³⁶ "Which of these three do you think was a neighbor to the man who fell into the hands of robbers?"

³⁷The expert in the law replied, "The one who had mercy on him."

Jesus told him, "Go and do likewise."

Are we to love and forgive these people that stole so much from us? Yes. If we want to be obedient to the Lord's words, yes.

It's taken us eight years to get to that point. In the beginning, there was so much pain and so much anger that there was no way we could have done what our Lord taught. Now, we pray for them every morning to repent. We pray that they will not face God's judgement. How can we pray this way? Ironically, we used to pray that they would face God's judgement, but Jesus has shown brightly through all that angst. He has softened our hearts. We weren't hurting them by feeling that way. We were hurting ourselves.

Chapter Sixteen

Living with Loss

"Sickness may befall, but the Lord will give grace; poverty may happen to us, but grace will surely be afforded; death must come but grace will light a candle at the darkest hour. Reader, how blessed it is as years roll round, and the leaves begin again to fall, to enjoy such an unfading promise as this, 'The Lord will give grace.'"[18]

Charles Spurgeon

When we were excommunicated and shunned there is one redeeming decision that we **did not** make. We did not reject what Jesus had done for us on the cross. When we came out, that's all I had. As I said earlier, I was hanging on to a splinter of the cross. I didn't know anything anymore except that Jesus loved me enough to die on the cross and shed His blood, so I could be forgiven of my sins. He became the ultimate sacrifice, so I would be able to have a relationship with the Father.

I knew all this, in my head, but it was rote. I had practiced the above dissertation since I was fourteen years old. Now, there was no emotion involved. I no longer "felt" the love of Christ. The concept was like a distant dream.

Emotion had been forbidden for twenty-three years. But I did hold on to that splinter. It was the only thing that got me through. That and Kevin spoon feeding me as he unraveled the false doctrine and compared it to the Word of God.

Jesus loved me when I accepted Him as Lord and Savior.

[18] http://www.reclaimingthemind.org/blog/2014/04/quotes-from-the-valley-of-the-shadow-of-death-charles-spurgeon-1834-1892/

Jesus loved me when I was in that cult and He loved me when I came out and didn't know which end was up. It didn't matter that I couldn't feel that love. I reckoned it as truth.

I was numb, and our relationship was one sided for a long time.

Many who leave a cult completely give up their beliefs in God. They don't know what to believe anymore so they run away from it all. Basically, they try to self-destruct. Those who leave have a hard time deciding what to eat, what to wear, how to choose those that can be trusted, how to make "any" type of decision for themselves.

There is a void that needs to be filled. The man that was making decisions for your life is no longer there. You can't find the Lord because He had been hidden from your sight for so many years. Now, you don't know where to look. What people decide to fill that void with varies from person to person. If there isn't counseling involved or a strong figure that represents a feasible plan, the person can lose complete control and fall in to whatever comes their way.

Also, more devastating than anything, the fear of possibly being disobedient is always just below the surface. Although you are free, the brainwashed mind continues to rule over logic. The program that was continually forced into your complete thought life keeps running through your mind over and over again.

"What if I do end up in Outer Darkness? What if I miss the Kingdom of God? What if the apostle really was the mouth piece of the Lord?"

The answer to these questions is...there is no definite

answer. As Christians, we depend on our faith, our love for God and our moral compass. We "trust" that the Holy Spirit will guide us along our way.

All the above have been compromised in our lives and we have lost our way. There is no direction and we are blind - not able to find the path.

As time rolls on and there is distance from leaving a cult, life becomes a little more comfortable. You tend to let your guard down just a bit. Everything can be just fine and then you see something on television or at a movie. Someone can trigger pain by saying a certain word. There may be a place that you visit that transports you right back to that prison where your hope was fettered.

You are similar to a prisoner of war with post - traumatic stress disorder. You can't eat, or you eat too much. You can't sleep, or you sleep too much. You're depressed, sometimes to the brink of suicidal thoughts.

These "triggers" that must be dealt with, usually, one at a time, tend to cripple and undermine any progress you might have made.

The above was true, especially in our case. We literally lost everything. I couldn't function. I couldn't make a decision for what to have for dinner. I wore the same thing all the time because I didn't want to have to think. I ate Panera's cinnamon bagels with walnut cream cheese by the dozen and put on I don't know how many pounds. And yes, I drank. It was beer at first then wine.

Why didn't I have enough faith to trust the Lord to help me? Because I was having a spiritual crisis about who He was. I had seen Jesus through the "apostle's" eyes for so long, my sight was blurred, and I couldn't trust my vision.

I'm not sanctifying my decisions. I knew they were wrong. I needed something to dull the pain of losing all my children and grandchildren within a week's time. It was either that or getting in the car and driving into that brick wall.

When this group had your children, it wasn't a transient ordeal. It was for good. Only a miracle could bring them out. Only a miracle could get you through that magnitude of loss, intact.

I'm sure there are some super Christians out there who will judge me. That's ok. I know my Lord Jesus forgave and forgives and is patient. My statement has nothing to do with "free grace". It's about two people, children of the King who were run over by a defrauded Mack truck. We were pieces lying all over the floor.

A writer and minister, dear to my heart, writes about pain. He writes about loss. He also writes about being found and loved and then changed to receive the "furious love of God." Brennan Manning understood the despondency of doubt and failure. But he also understood grace and mercy. He didn't write to excuse sin. He wrote to encourage us to find God in our fallen state and receive His love, for a purpose. That purpose is to be changed by it.

He used to say, "The Lord Jesus is going to ask each of us one question and only one question. He's going to ask you: Do you believe that I loved you? That I desired you? That I waited for you day after day? That I longed to hear the sound of your voice?"[19]

How we answer this question will determine how we perceive God. Do we believe He is conditional in delving out His love according to our actions? Or do we perceive

[19] katdish.net/2009/07/did-you-believe-that-i-loved-you-4

168

that He loves us unconditionally even when we are far away from Him?

The parable of the Prodigal Son should be the answer to this dilemma. The father loved his son without ceasing and unconditionally the whole time he was away and rejoiced when he returned home.

We had been living under conditional love for so many years, it was hard to see the Lord differently. It took me years to make that transition. But when I finally saw Him for who He truly is. I knew it was time for me to come home.

If there is no one there to help you in your transition in leaving a cult, to offer a leg up, more than not, futility is your future. But, don't give up! Your stepping stone just might be right around the corner.

"I respect you more than anyone I know. I'm so proud of you." Kevin said.

"What do you mean?"

"You have your periods when you're knocked back down and the loss is too much to bear but you seem to find a way to get back up. You don't stay there. You don't let insanity overtake you. You're strong, Darlin'. You always have been. It's strength, strength that the Lord has given you. That's what drew me to you from the beginning."

That's the special relationship we have. We're there to reach down our hands, each of us, into the abyss of loss and pull each other back up, out of the darkness, from the spinning madness of grief. It's a tough journey, but we always seem to make it back to the land of the living.

We haven't always been this strong. There were often times that we drove the car on pitch black, curvy roads, in the middle of nowhere, way over the speed limit, hoping the car would find its way to some immovable object. As I said, we wanted to go together. Neither of us would dare leave the other with such an insufferable burden to bear.

Now, I can be sitting on the couch crocheting, watching TV and this uncontrollable wave of sobs will unexpectedly come rising up from the deepest part of who I am. I'm suddenly conscious of my womb, where I carried my babies and birthed them into their existence. I try to be inconspicuous, not wanting to upset Kevin, but he sees me out of the corner of his eye.

"What's wrong?!"

I can't speak. The sobs stifle my words. He walks over and sits down next to me, drawing me to his chest, "The kids?"

I nod an affirmation. All he can do is hold me and pray. And he does pray and begs God for this to pass. But this bursting forth of raw pain always lasts through the night. When the sun rises, I gain strength in the light of a new day. We begin again.

The pain is never that far from the surface. I carry it every day, in prayer, in memories, in hope of change. And without our faith, I wouldn't be here, neither would Kevin.

My babies – don't want to have anything to do with Kevin or me. My flesh and blood the children I gave birth to, don't want to talk, remember, love us....anymore. The midnight hour is a vicious place to be. Will sleep come? Will I be relieved of this torment? I wait. I hear the clock on the wall ticking away the seconds, the minutes, the hours. Will I receive respite? Will tomorrow bring comfort?

Rachel and I have a lot in common.

"A voice is heard in Ramah, mourning and great weeping, Rachel weeping for her children and refusing to be comforted, because they are no more." Jeremiah 31:15 NKJV

What do you do when you have to choose between the Lord and your children?

What about if the day comes when you must choose between the Lord and your life?

Is there a difference?

Recently, Kevin and I were staying with his sister and her husband. We were there for Easter and they wanted us to go to church with them that Sunday. Kevin and I were up for it. We hadn't been to church since we were going to "our" church - the one we built. We were renting it out to a terrific pastor and his wife and we were going to his services. Then, we moved away. So, it had been a while.

As soon as my brother-in-law drove up to the door to let us out, I began to feel strange. The greeters were at the door and they shook our hands and welcomed us. I tried to smile but couldn't say a word. Kevin held my hand and we walked through the double doors into a building that had a long wide hallway that led to the sanctuary.

As we got closer I could hear the worship leaders singing – then the congregation – then we walked through the main door to the sanctuary. Something was happening to me that I had absolutely no control over.

I hurried to sit down by my sister-in-law. Kevin was still out in the foyer. I felt so uncomfortable. My sister-in-law called a friend over and they started talking about grandchildren. When her friend said, "I just bought my grand-daughter her first pair of high heels," that pushed me over the edge. I got up to walk out. There was that visceral response happening with my emotions. The only way I can describe this feeling is, it is like when you literally have to throw up, but this was of the mind not physically. Just how it's uncontrollable physically, it was uncontrollable mentally. I knew I was going to explode and I had to get to that door. I ran into Kevin as he was coming in.

"What's wrong?" I couldn't speak at first them I whispered, "Please - Take me to the bathroom."

He put his arm around me as the flood of tears and emotion came pouring out. We were passing people as we walked, and I held my head down hoping and praying that they wouldn't see my face.

We finally made it to the bathroom and when I walked through the door, a culmination of thoughts and memory came rushing into my brain. Sobs broke free from deep inside of me and I was stranded there for I don't know how long.

Finally, I began to calm down. I was feeling somewhat better. I just wanted to get to Kevin. He has always been my pinnacle of strength. I came out of the door, "What happened?" he asked, "Was it the kids?"

I explained to him the best that I could. We hadn't been in a church for a while and just the atmosphere stimulated something deep inside of me. Then, of course, I was thinking about my children and grandchildren and our life when they were still a part of it. Being there without them, when they had been such an intricate part of when we went to "church", was too much.

It was an avalanche of memories and emotion. I also remembered the atmosphere of the cult we were in. I remembered how my stomach used to churn when we would get close to the building when we were driving to services on Sunday morning.

We couldn't leave because we had driven there with Kevin's sister and brother-in-law. So, we quietly entered the sanctuary and headed to the back. We found two seats and sat down right away. The preaching was winding up and there was an announcement about the congregation partaking of Communion.

We sat tight. We just wanted to be invisible. Then I saw my sister and brother-in-law walking toward us with the most touching gesture. They were holding communion wafers and tiny vials of grape juice. Kevin immediately shook his head and said, "No."

"You don't want it?" his sister asked.

"No", he reiterated.

"I will", I said and took the offering.

They went back to their seats and I turned to Kevin and asked why he didn't partake. He said he was too angry. At first, I thought he was upset with me, but then he explained that it was our "kids". He couldn't partake of the Lord's Supper when he witnessed what had happened to me. It had stirred some dormant thoughts about all we had been through and the unbelief that our own children were a part of it.

It has been said time heals all wounds. I do not agree. The wounds remain. In time, the mind protecting its sanity covers them with scar tissue and the pain lessens, but it is never gone.[20]

Rose Kennedy

[20] https://www.brainyquote.com/quotes/rose_kennedy_597699

I wish I could tell you that there is eventually victory that we attain in the loss of our children and grandchildren. I wish I could write to you about some supernatural solution to such a horrific and terrible loss. But I can't. What I can tell you is that we have found the definition of what overcoming truly means. The Bible is replete with scripture about overcoming.

They will fight against you but will not overcome you, for I am with you and will rescue you," declares the LORD. Jeremiah 1:19 NKJV

We, as flesh, see a time of victory in overcoming. We think they are two in the same. We're wrong. Overcoming is a process and ongoing. Victory is a culmination. Our directive is to continue to overcome despite loss, in spite of vanquished hopes and unfulfilled dreams. Why? Because our journey is a continuation of overcoming and our destination is a final victory in Christ Jesus.

Chapter Seventeen

At the End of the Day

"I would go to the deeps a hundred times to cheer a downcast spirit. It is good for me to have been afflicted, that I might know how to speak a word in season to one that is weary."[21]

Charles Spurgeon

"Good night Honey," says Kevin. "I'm going to bed."

"Alright."

"I love you more than life."

"I love "you" more than life."

"I don't know where I'd be without you."

"Me too."

We comfort each other. We have been doing so for over thirty-six years now. The last ten years, paradoxically, have brought us closer together, oh, so much closer.

He has to work tomorrow. I'm left with my thoughts. I'm alone. All the "what ifs" and the "if only" come flooding in.

The fact that we made a decision to stay in that cult - The fact that we made a decision to even visit haunts my very soul.

It's very rare to leave this place or any cult without loss. What you lose is always priceless. Very few leave whole.

Amos 3:12 NKJ tells about a shepherd who retrieves from the lion's mouth two legs or a piece of an ear. That is usually what is left when you leave a cult – when you leave "this" cult.

21 https://www.goodreads.com/author/quotes/2876959.Charles_Haddon_Spurgeon

But the Good Shepherd takes what is left and molds the remains into His plan, His calling – IF you allow Him. You must be able to recognize Him as "The" Shepherd to allow such transformation. Very few do. They remain what is left in the lion's mouth and refuse the Shepheard's help. They limp through life cripple and deaf.

Although some families escape intact, the poison that has seeped in from this place is lethal. These families that are looking forward to freedom and liberty find they are still fettered by the corruption of the "religious law" -legalism and heresy. Couples who were unconditionally in love with one another, feel like strangers. Young people find themselves insecure and unworthy of any kind of success – future. There are phobias developed, futures snuffed out and faiths destroyed.

I make jewelry, sell jewelry and beads, write books, do photography, crochet and work as an RN. I try to keep my mind so occupied that I can't think.

Why didn't we stay out when we left that time? What made us go back?... Our children.

Who stayed in when we left for good?... Our children.

I look at my husband, in the evenings, sitting across from me on the couch in our living room. The fire is going in the fireplace, Fox News is on the television, I see his face and remember. I go back thirty-five – forty years and he is there. He's loved me since he was sixteen and the Lord kept him... for me.

He was there for me and my little girl when we needed him, he took us both in and made us his own. He endeavored to be obedient to the Lord's calling. He tried to be a good pastor and work full time to support his family. I don't know why it happened to be for a cult – why it was all for naught. Why did we lose so much? We'll know soon. Our lives are close to coming to an end. He's the most kind, patient, generous person I know. These last ten years have focused him to perceive what is really important – me the Lord and his children – not necessarily in that order. His highest priority is to keep me sane, to keep me safe and to fulfill my forgotten dreams. He is truly my knight in shining armor. He doesn't deserve the rumors, that are held as truth, in the remaining churches that are left in this cult.

It appears that none of them are getting what *they* deserve. But, "'Vengeance is Mine,' saith the Lord". We're content with that.

Prayer Finally Answered

It's been ten years now since we have been out of the cult. Days keep slipping by revealing what will be. After two and a half years, I'm near the culmination of this book.

Not long ago, I was sitting at the nail spa getting my nails done when my phone rang. I looked down at the caller ID and saw the city where the call was coming from. My heart jumped into my throat.

"Hello?"

"Mom?"

"Oh, Sweetheart!" I started sobbing. It was my eldest. She had left the cult a month prior and was now calling me. Her voice was shaking, and she was in tears. We talked for I don't know how long.

When we finally hung up, I was so excited! I had to call

Kevin!! He was ecstatic! Then I called everyone that had prayed with me and for me these past ten years.

The call came in November. We got together Christmas with her, our son-in-law and three grandchildren that we hadn't seen in ten years. What a homecoming!

We talked on the phone every day from when she called me at the nail salon. We both were looking forward to the day, we would finally see one another again. I was hoping and praying our love for each other would pick up from where it left off!

When their car drove into the driveway on that December afternoon, a few days before Christmas, it barely stopped when she was out the door and running into my arms.

Kevin and I stood and embraced everyone of them as they filed out of the car. My son-in-law was next. He has always had a special place in my heart and that place was instantly filled again. Our grandchildren had grown up. How many moments we had lost but, how many moments will be gained. And, we will not take them for granted.

Christmas was surreal! The best Christmas ever! We sat and talked for hours in my sister-in law's den downstairs. It was just the seven of us. Our grandchildren began to know us again. It was as if they never left!

They have now moved back home, to where we are living. They live only ten minutes away and we see each other all the time. Kevin and I have been able to celebrate Mother's Day and Father's Day, birthdays and holidays for the first time since they left.

When the Lord answers prayer it is always so much beyond what you ever thought it would be.

The ten years have elapsed in time. Yet, He has redeemed the years that the cankerworm had eaten away with our daughter! God is truly the Lord of reconciliation! Our grandchildren are now twenty, seventeen and thirteen. Kevin and I are spending a lot of time with them and we are on Cloud Nine!. I talk with our daughter almost every day. I hold on to the following promise:

Isaiah 61:3 NKJV :
He has sent me (Isaiah)... to appoint to those who mourn in Zion, to give to them a **garland** for **ashes**, the oil of joy for mourning (and) the garment of praise for the spirit of heaviness;

One Year Later

In the great promise of the above scripture there are rays of hope yet, mottled in the darkness.

Will there be garland?

There is a reason I didn't publish this book when it was finished a year ago. The Lord wasn't finished with what He wanted me to say.

I wish this could be the happy ending for all of us, the one we all wish for. But the reality is...although the Lord is able, the damage is done. Those who have experienced the toxic life style and accepted the ways of a cult, are forever altered.

Post traumatic stress syndrome, depression, loss of the authentic self, self-doubt, questionable relationship with the Lord, mistrust.

Every negative result mentioned in the above paragraph,

and even so much more, is what is left in the wake of a cult. I have found the quote below to be just as true as scripture.

[1]**Evil** is both harmful and inexplicable, but not just that; what defines an **evil** act is that it is permanently disorienting for all those touched by it.

Our other two children, their spouses and seven grandchildren remain within the confines of what our Lord Jesus died to free them from. Legalism, man driven doctrine, control, fear, elitism and shunning are all aspects of what Jesus fought against with the Pharisee.

We have all been touched by these evil acts and there is an aftermath of dysfunction. So, what is the answer?

We may need help in finding ourselves again. Look for someone who can be trusted. Find someone who will validate that you don't need to be told what decisions you should make. In my case, Kevin and I get together regularly with our daughter and her family. We lift one another up in prayer. We encourage one another and allow our love for each other to overtake what damage has been done.

Most of all, we continue to hang on to Jesus. We focus and reaffirm daily, that He is our First Love. We don't give up and let the evil overtake us. We crawl little by little back to the cross and what God established *there*.

I have come to the conclusion that doctrine doesn't matter, tradition doesn't matter, leadership in any form, doesn't matter. All that matters is, Jesus defeated death. He defeated evil on that cross. He established the beginning of His Kingdom on this earth. The culmination being when He comes back again. His resurrection is proof.

So...If you are at a point where you can't embrace the cross with all that is within you, then look for a splinter, just a splinter of the cross. When you see it...take it, no matter how small...put it in your hand ... be thankful ... and ... hold on!